Praise for *The Joy of Uber Dr*

"*The Joy of Uber Driving* is a wild, nostalgic
weaves true tales from her Uber driving expe.
blended with her life-review-in-the-rearview-mirror stories. It skillfully
blends humor, warmth, pathos, insight, and inspiration . . . and, at the
very least, will give you an enormous respect for your next Uber driver."
—Kelly Sullivan Walden, dream expert and best-selling coauthor
of *Chicken Soup for the Soul: Dreams and Premonitions*

"This is a portrait of one woman's journey into self-love that will reach
to the very core of every woman's heart. The raw honesty and insight
Yamini shares with us through her challenges and interactions ignites
the spark of hope in all of us. And you'll be taken over by her unexpected humor and her lightheartedness. Take the joyful ride and read
this book—it will delight you!"
—Agapi Stassinopoulos, best-selling author of
Wake Up to the Joy of You

"Yamini has turned up the volume on her extraordinary life. You'll be
riveted by this memoir. Her storytelling is at times intensely raw and
insightful and at other times unexpectedly hilarious as she weaves in
meaningful Uber stories with her own personal stories."
—Jill Lublin, international speaker and
four-time best-selling author

"Uber drivers and passengers will enjoy the escapades of Yamini
Redewill as riders reveal their deep inner longings in the backseat of
her Prius. Sometimes 'therapist' and sometimes 'cheerleader,' Redewill
touches hearts as she shares stories from the lives of her passengers,
along with her own roller coaster journey to fulfillment."
—Randy Peyser, author of *Crappy to Happy*

"Yamini Redewill takes us on an insightful ride into her creative
world, interweaving her life experiences with those of her passengers.
A MUST READ!"
—Judith Morton Fraser, LMFT, author of
What's So Good About "Bad" Feelings? and *Grandmas Never Die*

THE JOY OF UBER DRIVING

THE JOY OF UBER DRIVING

A WILD RIDE TO SELF-LOVE

YAMINI REDEWILL

SHE WRITES PRESS

Published June 2019
Printed in the United States of America
Print ISBN: 978-1-63152-567-4
E-ISBN: 978-1-63152-568-1
Library of Congress Control Number: 2019932779

For information, address:
She Writes Press
1569 Solano Ave #546
Berkeley, CA 94707

She Writes Press is a division of SparkPoint Studio, LLC.

Names and identifying characteristics have been changed to protect the privacy of certain individuals.

Dedication

At this time, it has become clear to me that I wrote this book as an incentive for women who feel abused, unworthy, and unable to defend themselves against the misogynous tyranny that has existed for centuries. The fact that it has become the big news of the day fits perfectly with my life's purpose and the work I have done through my art as my contribution to the awakening of our society toward justice, equality, and self-love.

I dedicate this book to the #MeToo movement, even though I claim complicity as a victim because of my upbringing, which blinded me to the truth of this inequity. My victimhood ran very deep and affected every aspect of my life unknowingly until my life lessons and spiritual teachers led me to the truth of who I am. I hope there will be some who recognize something of themselves in my story.

I also dedicate this book to the Uber Corporation, which has provided myself and thousands of single women over fifty the opportunity to be self-sufficient in a totally equitable and supportive way.

CONTENTS

INTRODUCTION

As an Uber driver since 2015, I realize that I have a special mission: to be a source of light and levity touching every one of my passengers with truth, humor, and unconditional love. I always thought I was going to do it on a grand scale, with dreams of fame and fortune as a singer/actress using beautiful words and lyrics written by someone else. But it was not meant to be. Instead, I'm able to impact a few people at a time on a personal level with the love and wisdom I've gained through years of conscious learning and practice. And now, I'm using Uber to deliver my memoir interspersed with intriguing personal stories from my passengers that coincide with my own stories. I've named each chapter after a song from the sixties, seventies, and eighties because of my deep love of music and the meaningful songs of that period.

Being an Uber driver has opened up a whole new world to me where I relate to people of all ages and ethnicities and recognize that "they are me." I have witnessed real and meaningful transformations in short periods of time through our interactions. These sacred moments in time give me hope that humanity is malleable and open to becoming more and more conscious. It has also given me a vehicle for my own transformation in that I'm able to stop myself from judging my riders or making assumptions about them before giving them a chance to reveal their true nature.

As shame fueled generations of women to not speak up, my story begins with a natural setup for feminine shame: when I was born, the name I was given was Frances Hamilton Redewill after my father and my grandfather, because I was supposed to be a boy, Francis Hamilton Redewill III. They never even stopped to consider a girl's name, but at least they changed it from Francis to Frances to comply with my gender. I believe that was the origin of my shame as a woman. As an adult many years later, my name would be changed by my spiritual master, Bhagwan Shree Rajneesh, later known as Osho. He gave me the name Yamini, meaning "going beyond the night" into a life of consciousness.

The second incidence of shame to influence my behavior came as a result of my father being a chauvinistic womanizer who chased (literally) after other women in front of my mother and me and treated these women as though they were far more important and interesting than my mother. I grew up thinking this kind of behavior was normal and that I could be interesting only as a sex object to men in order to get love or success as the singer/actress I'd dedicated myself to becoming. Beneath these thoughts was the subconscious belief that if I got married, I would end up being ignored and unloved just as my mother was.

Writing this memoir has made me connect the dots to so many seemingly incongruent events. I realized that the bulk of my life has been about plunging head first into situations with blind passion and either loving the consequences or, after a period of grief, accepting failures as lessons for my growth. It's also been about making the choice to live *my* life, not somebody else's. I can say, without hesitation, that by most standards, the choices I made in my twenties were from a reckless, scattered, unconscious, self-centered, and a low-self-esteem frame of mind. In my thirties and forties, I was an unhappy and confused spiritual seeker who was unlucky at love but unwittingly lucky to land a job as head of wardrobe at CBS, and I found my spiritual center. My fifties and sixties brought me to a place of many forms of creativity and leadership training in which I experienced new avenues of success and a new perception of what was possible for my life. However, I was still single and alone and not totally okay with it. Finally, in my seventies, I found the truth of who I am, why I am, and how true happiness and a youthful spirit has evolved and defined this woman known as Yamini.

As you read my story, you will discover that this is not a "how-to" book giving you everything you need to get skinnier, live longer, look younger, or become financially rich and successful. It's also not an epic love story with a Hollywood ending. It's more like an *Eat, Pray, Love* mixed with a *What the Bleep Do We Know?* kind of story that reveals the inner workings of a perpetually single woman, manifesting sometimes devastating, usually melodramatic, but always spiritually relevant events in her life that bring her closer to true happiness along with the existential joy of Uber driving. It is the unfolding of a bona fide #MeToo-er who evolved into a loving and self-loved woman.

Our whole world is reeling and careening out of control as, more and more, we are witnessing violent actions caused from psychiatric issues within our fragile society. I was moved to tears by Oprah Winfrey's speech at the 2018 Golden Globes. This icon filled the massive black hole in all our lives created by our insane president who dominates the news every day with one hellish bombshell after another. As "A new day is on the horizon!" was forcefully proclaimed by Oprah and tears poured from my eyes, I realized how much we needed to hear her impassioned speech and tell our stories and be witnessed.

I listen to my Uber passengers' stories. I hear some of their deepest longings. And so, knowing what is needed now, I am offering my memoir as a tribute to all the #MeToo-ers who have stood up and told their truth, and to all the ones who will stand up in the future, and to all the men who have daughters who care about their futures, and to all the good men who truly know a woman's worth and honor it.

Hallelujah! A new day is on the horizon!

FOREVER YOUNG

May Your Wishes All Come True!

It has now been over two years since I signed up to be an Uber driver in the Bay Area in 2015, and it is with an ironic sense of pride that I tell my friends and acquaintances, "I'm an Uber driver." After seventy-eight years on this planet, navigating the corkscrew twists and turns of my life from a privileged but unhappy childhood, through failures and successes and extramarital affairs in Hollywood, to experimental immersions into various forms of spirituality and personal empowerment workshops, I now find myself uncommonly happy as a single woman, driving twenty-plus hours a week for Uber.

From the time I was a seven-year-old girl named Frances, as an aspiring singer and actress, I perceived that the spotlight was always on *me*. My reality was more like a movie, with improvised scripts, a soundtrack, supporting actors, and an audience following me everywhere on my way to stardom. I could never have imagined that instead of being a famous singer or movie star, I would end up behind the wheel of my own glorified taxicab. How could I know that when I grew up, instead of playing in large movie houses, I would be ad-libbing to a captured audience of one to four people about seven times a day? But more often than not, I would be listening to my back-seat audience and receiving wisdom and insight on a daily basis. Being an

Uber driver has taught me the valuable lesson of deep listening and relating to each passenger on an intuitive level. I have come to believe that every encounter is an important thread in my life's tapestry. However brief and however subtle, each one provides a new awareness of myself and my interconnection to all living things, edging me closer and closer to the truth of who I am.

Throughout my childhood I didn't feel I fit anywhere, so I found comfort in my daydreams and on the stage, with stage lights separating me from everyone else. Consciousness had a circuitous route in my life, and only when I came close to suicide did it round the corner to meet me. Until then, nothing in my life worked or made sense, least of all *love*.

Do you remember when you drove your first car? Did the unmistakable feeling of power and freedom mesmerize you like it did me? Did you think anything was possible for your life back then? I know when I clutched the wheel of my mom's '55 red-and-white Chevy Bel-Air convertible in the summer of my fifteenth year and pulled out of the driveway with my hair waving wildly in the wind, I thought I was going in a straight line to fame and fortune. I had the looks, the hair, the talent, and the smarts. *My daddy's rich and my mama's good lookin'.* What could possibly go wrong?

The most exasperating but wonderful thing about life is that it is unscripted and unpredictable but always open for re-interpretations and rewrites. Little did I know then how many twists and turns it would take to hurtle me from one set of realities to another in order to grow me into the person I was destined to become (and am still becoming).

All I knew at that age was that I was a gifted artist, singer, and actress, loving all the attention and applause I got. It was obvious to me that being on stage was my ticket to happiness. Applause after every song—that's what happiness was all about! Being narcissistically optimistic, I honestly believed that was all that I needed to achieve supreme happiness, judging from all the happy Hollywood endings in the movies I loved. How could I know that in the real world, this was a path that would lead to long-term depression and near self-destruction?

PING! (This is the sound my Uber app makes when I'm being summoned by a potential rider). I was directed to the financial district near Market Street where a young girl named Lorelei in her early twenties stood. As I drove up, she hopped into the back seat and we exchanged greetings. Soon, she started rummaging through a large bag and drew out a slinky black dress and some flashy jewelry. To my amazement, she pulled down her brown wool leggings, pulled off her sweater, and then wriggled into the dress rather dexterously in the small back-seat area. She seemed unconcerned about possible gawkers. She then replaced her walking shoes with spike heels and stuffed her work clothes in the bag. Breathlessly, after achieving this feat in record time, she apologized and then began to perform a hair and makeup do-over. While applying eyeliner, she explained that she was going to audition as a singer at a well-known club on Broadway and she was very nervous. (For those who don't know San Francisco, Broadway is in North Beach and has rows of strip clubs). Without makeup, she was a naturally pretty girl crowned with copper-colored hair tied in a knot, who looked too sweet and naive to be in that environment. I mentioned that I had been a singer myself once, and she said, "Oh really? How exciting! Were you with a band?"

I shook my head, "No, not really."

I told her about my life as an aspiring actress and singer in Hollywood and then told her to be very careful, as people are not always what they seem. "The best thing to do is follow your gut instinct and be true to yourself. If they want you to do something that doesn't feel right, chances are it isn't."

I watched as she artfully transformed herself into a striking beauty with large, green, doe-like eyes and long wavy hair cascading over her shoulders. When I let her off at her destination, I wished her well, and she thanked me and told me not to worry. She disappeared, spike heels and all, into what I would call a black hole on Broadway. I whispered a silent prayer for her and answered another *ping*.

Being an Uber driver can sometimes turn you into a surrogate therapist, a counselor, a cheerleader, a mother, a friend, or just a listening post. At my age, I have a depth of experience to draw from, and because my life has been filled with so many wildly diverse situations, I seem to be able to relate to a large number of people in a personal way. It is an honor to be of service in this manner every day, and every day brings new adventures and new possibilities for my own reflection and growth. I hope I meet this girl again one day and find out if she succeeded as an entertainer and stayed true to herself.

One aspect of my life I hadn't counted on being in the way of my happiness was my inability to form intimate relationships with men. Naturally, when my happiest moments were on stage in a surreal and brightly colored fake setting and a readymade script, coming face to face with common reality up close in broad daylight was unappealing and inherently boring. To appease the situation and spice up my reality with a little drama, I often played the part of Bette Davis's Jezebel, pushing boys away who got too close (especially pimply-faced ones).

Somewhere around thirteen years of age I remember screaming with the passion of a caged wild animal, "I can't be anything to anybody until I love myself!" This was directed at my domineering grandmother, who was intent on making a lady out of me by teaching me to be all things to all people. I had forgotten this episode until just recently, and now I clearly recognize it as a declaration of my soul's purpose for living and possibly helping others learn how to love themselves. Ten years ago my passion for empowering women to love themselves was revealed to me through my photography. I particularly focused on women over forty and dressed them in long flowing gowns with chiffon scarves to dance or pose with in nature. I saw that an authentic feminine beauty and strength emerged as they related to nature symbiotically.

I'm compelled to mention a little more about my "domineering" grandmother after reading an old news article about her being heralded as an up-and-coming concert pianist in Parisian social circles in her mid-twenties. She married my grandfather in 1910 after knowing him for less than a month. What a woman! Later she and Grandpa ended up in the Bay Area, where he practiced medicine. She was a close friend of Clara Clemens, the daughter of Mark Twain, whom she met in Vienna, where they were both students of music. This all helped me to understand her insistence on teaching me the social graces. Perhaps if I hadn't been so defiant, I would have also married early in life—that is, if I could overcome my fear of marriage as a deterrent to happiness.

I consider myself lucky that I actually stood up to her, whereas my dad could not as a young boy and did not as a young man. He suffered enumerable assaults on his manhood by this woman who, among other things, made the mistake of dying his only pair of corduroy pants pink and forcing him to wear them throughout his senior year of high school (this was during the 1930's depression). The ripple effect was a dad who I have disparaged throughout this book as a selfish, egotistical womanizer. He may have been, but I'm here to counter those accusations with the fact that I am a chip off the old block. He is my mirror. He is the part of me that I used to sabotage my happiness and later used as an excuse, which I could complain about in one personal growth workshop after another. If I have a Twin Flame, I would guess he is it. We were so much alike, and I was always "Daddy's girl." From the time I was seven, he was there coaching me and doing everything he could to help me fulfill my dreams. God bless you, Daddy. Just know how much I love you and please forgive me for writing this book.

2

MY HEART BELONGS TO DADDY
So Take a Hike, Laddie

Prepared for another fabulous day of Uber driving, I turned on my cell phone and clicked on the Uber app to say I was available and ready to work.

I offered a prayer of intention to serve for the highest good. I sat with eyes closed, windows up, engine off, as I chanted my familiar but heartfelt mantra: "I accept myself as an aspect of the Creator in full manifestation. I align every aspect of my being to this truth. I know who I am, I know what I am, and I know how I serve. I serve with joy, love, great gratitude, and the highest intentions so that all who enter this car may feel safe, appreciated, happy, and perhaps just a little inspired to know and love themselves more. Thank you, Mother Father God, for allowing me this opportunity to serve and to grow. Thank you for this beautiful day on Planet Earth."

I opened my eyes, pressed the engine button, and quietly pulled out of my parallel parking space in front of my house when . . .

PING! I was summoned to a house on a steep windy one-lane street in Mill Valley, where a guy named Darren stood with stooped shoulders and a downcast expression. He opened the door and half-heartedly said "Hi . . . thanks for picking me up." I inquired as to where he was headed, and he simply said, "My therapist in the city."

There was a long pause followed by a deep sigh, then I finally asked, "How are you?"

Tentatively he said, "Miserable and a little paranoid."

Sensing he may want to vent his feelings, I asked, "Do you want to talk about it?"

I was actually surprised when he brightened and said, "Yes!" and exclaimed, "Have you ever felt like everyone in your life is in on a joke about you?"

"Uh . . . no, I don't think so. What do you mean?"

"Well, it feels like I'm a laughing stock. I don't know, it just seems everyone is judging me and whispering behind my back and maliciously snickering."

Cautiously, I queried, "I'm so sorry. What happened that makes you think that?"

"Oh, nothing in particular. Maybe it's because I'm thirty-five and living with my parents. They don't understand. I have been trying really hard to find a job and get out on my own again, but the jobs offered don't pay enough to live here."

Oh-oh . . . I felt my social worker self and all my years of spiritual training coming on and just couldn't resist the temptation. I went headlong into the fray and offered my own experience to ease him into a new reality: "You know what? I remember when I also went home to live with my mother in my thirties and thought everyone was judging me behind my back, only to find out later that I had imagined the whole thing when I confronted them about it."

"Wow!" he said, amazed. "My therapist had the same experience and came up with the same conclusion. He said our thoughts create our reality. Is that what you're trying to tell me?"

I smiled and nodded.

Squinting suspiciously, he said, "Are you two in cahoots?"

I laughed. "Oh, come on, stop with the paranoia already!"

He lightened up and began going into great detail about all the jobs he had applied for and why they were not what he wanted. I asked what he really wanted, to which he replied with another fifteen minutes of rhapsodic descriptions and calculations of a future he passionately desired. We arrived at his destination and his face showed a far different countenance with shining eyes and color in his cheeks. He left thanking me for letting him talk and said he felt much better.

I thought, *Thank you, God, for reminding me that my own reality is a mirror of my thoughts and then giving me the opportunity to fortify his therapist's work with my experience. That's what* "Ubering" is all about.

In 1957 I was accepted at Cal Berkeley as a legacy candidate. I transferred to UCLA in 1960 because of their great art and drama departments, but I dropped out in my senior year. Prior to leaving UCLA, you could say I was a passenger in my life. My parents firmly gripped the wheel, providing me with all the financial support I needed and guiding my choices with a certain amount of appreciated parental wisdom. However, Mom and Dad got a divorce the day I entered college, which called their wisdom into question. The fact that they waited so long to divorce proved a lack of wisdom from my point of view, but it also proved how unselfish and caring they were toward me, to wait until I was safely out of the house.

I was born into a life of privilege, as we were "nouveaux-riche," my dad being a new and popular pediatrician in Whittier. Early on, a local politician named Richard Nixon and his family became his regular patients. Years later, we had the (dubious) honor of visiting Nixon in his DC office when he became Eisenhower's vice president. People in DC thought he was the "Golden Boy" at that time. Interesting how time changes perceptions when one's true nature is revealed.

Dad was energetically outgoing, and flamboyant, and loved being the center of attention, oftentimes doing impromptu performances on his squeaky violin or slapping his big bass fiddle. Mother was quiet and reserved, always in the background, and chronically unhappy. Dad thrived on collecting status symbols such as a large three-story house with a pool in Whittier, another house in the desert, one at the beach, a cabin in the mountains, and later, an apartment in Avalon. He also had a penchant for buying a new car every six months, which ranged from European sports cars to Cadillac sedans, much to my mother's constant frustration at not being able to coax him into buying the needed paint job and repairs for the house in Whittier.

In a sense, Mom was also a status symbol, being the daughter of Frederick Johnson, the president of Bell Telephone in Canada at the time. Dad and Mom met at McGill University in Montreal when he was in med school. I always had the feeling that "Nan and Grandy Johnson" looked down their noses at my dad, thinking him to be the opportunist that he, in fact, was. My grandfather, who looked exactly like King George, Queen Elizabeth's father, intrigued me. He carried himself regally, with one hand behind on the small of his back as he walked down the hill to his office. They originally came from England, and when he became president of Bell Telephone of Canada, they were invited to dine with the queen at Buckingham Palace.

We visited them five times in my lifetime, once when I was four, then when I was eight or nine, again when I was fifteen, again in 1967 for the World's Fair, and lastly in my mid-thirties. On my first visit at the age of four, I embarrassed a dinner guest when I sat on her lap and asked why she wore two girdles. In the winter, the women congregate in the bedroom and adjust their clothes before coming to dinner. I was privy to the room, where I observed this strange tradition. I remember being immediately shuttled off to the attic, where I was left for about two hours. I yelled and cried and yelled, but nobody came. I was so angry I found a pair of scissors and cut one side of my long ash blond hair off. That is the only negative memory I have of Montreal.

They had a large apartment on Cote des Neiges with a maid who was also their cook and Andy the chauffeur, who picked us up in New York when I was fifteen and drove us to Montreal. I remember having oatmeal served in a beautiful bone china bowl and a fine linen napkin adorned with a silver serviette holder, and from that time forward, oatmeal mush was a delicacy to me.

The truth is, I was embarrassed by our show of wealth, as almost all my school friends were far less well to do. When I was gifted with my first car on my sixteenth Christmas, I was depressed, convinced that I wouldn't be liked by my peers, because I was the first girl to own a car in my high school. It didn't help that it was an ugly old black '39 Nash. It turned out I became more popular for the very reason I thought the other girls would hate me: I had a car.

I think part of my mom's sadness came from feeling like a wall-flower whenever she and Dad were around other women. My dad openly flirted and later succumbed to having affairs with some of them. I caught him on a couple of occasions, fondling a female guest in the darkened kitchen while a party commenced in the living room, or kissing a guest outside by the pool, which was far removed from the house. Our next-door neighbor was a particular threat to Mom, but being that it was in the mid-fifties, nothing was ever spoken of or alluded to. The grownups all knew how to hide their feelings and suspicions quite well while pretending to have perfect marriages and to be the best of friends with each other.

My poor mother really had no one to talk to about anything relevant or important, such as her feelings about my dad. It just wasn't done. She came from an old-world English family whose very conservative values placed importance on good manners and social mores. Consequently, she was not able to express herself or defend herself when arguing with my dad, which they did on a regular basis in angry hushed tones behind closed doors. As for showing affection toward each other, I remember them kissing only once when he came home from work. I thought it strange but nice at the time. More importantly, she was unable to show outward affection toward me. I don't remember her ever hugging me or comforting me when I was sad or hurt as a child. Maybe she did, I just can't seem to remember.

She was not a mean woman. She was gentle and kind and had a good heart, just not overtly affectionate. She once confessed to me that she had been in love with someone else, but Dad swept her off her feet, and before she knew what happened, they were married. She told me she was glad, because otherwise she never would have had me (she said with a wistful sigh).

Her bottled-up rage toward my dad turned into severe migraine headaches that lasted for weeks. I remember her often lying in bed in a darkened room with an icepack on her forehead. I had to learn to cook Dad's dinner every night during this time. She finally had a nervous breakdown, which resulted in an epileptic seizure while at a garden party. I believe the seizure partly came from the myriad drugs Dad prescribed for her. They eventually became her ultimate demise. Forty years later, she was taking fourteen drugs prescribed by two different doctors, which resulted in a massive stroke at the end of her life.

PING! **A woman named Jackie called from her doctor's office in Marin. When she emerged and approached my car, I saw a "mystery" woman I thought to be in her mid-fifties. She sported a wide-brimmed hat, big dark glasses, and a turtleneck sweater beneath a long black coat in the middle of summer. A bag full of prescription drugs rattled in the back seat beside her. It sounded as if she were opening each bottle and counting the capsules in the back seat while I drove the entire distance to her home twelve miles away. We didn't engage in a conversation until we got close to her home, and I asked what she did for a living. She said she had been a publicist but was basically retired now.**

As she spoke to me, she took off her sunglasses, and I was shocked to see a very young and beautiful woman. I asked her

why she was trying to hide, and she replied that she'd gained so much weight from her medications that her husband criticized her incessantly. A big alarm bell went off in my head as I recognized a common form of self-loathing felt by women with abusive husbands. I told her she was extremely beautiful and that maybe her husband should get glasses or, even better, see a psychiatrist. She shook her head, let out a derisive laugh, and murmured under her breath, "That'll be the day!"

Having arrived at her house, I stopped the car, turned off the engine, and turned around to face her. "I'm serious. You should look at yourself and see what I see. I know someone who might be able to help both of you see what I see." With that, I gave her a card of a personal friend who was a well-known marriage counselor and love therapist in the area. She looked at me in disbelief as she took the card from my hand. After a long pause, she smiled and said thank you and opened the door to leave. She stood there watching me as I drove away.

Going back to my father. I don't blame Dad for my mother's death. He only prescribed what he knew to be the best medicine at the time. However, his medical ignorance spilled over onto my thirtieth birthday when he announced, while dining at a restaurant he picked for my birthday, that I'd probably inherited my mother's epilepsy. It was a very strange and hurtful way of celebrating my birthday. He probably wasn't aware that her migraines and so-called epileptic seizures stopped the day she divorced him.

When I was ten, they adopted my baby brother, David. He was a diversion that served to forestall their eventual divorce. I don't remember much about him growing up. It wasn't until Mom died that we became close through our shared grief, and later, we helped our father through his transition.

David was, by nature, always a very private person, while I was all wrapped up in my self-absorbed dreams, leaving little room for anything or anyone else. We didn't share any interests or personal goals. We were strangers who lived in the same house, only barely aware of each other. We have since grown very fond of each other. Basically, he is my rock. I know I can depend on him in a pinch.

My shadowy impression of my dad started at the age of four while we were in Phoenix visiting our relatives. I'd been put in a guestroom for bed that night when suddenly the door flew open. There was Dad, chasing one of my aunts. He pounced on her in a drunken stupor and pulled her dress over her head. Several people rushed into the room and dragged him away from her. I don't remember anyone being concerned that I had witnessed the whole shocking incident. I think I pretended to be asleep. So it was that I came to expect this kind of behavior from my father as being normal. I think it also colored my opinion of men in general. It's normal for them to act like animals around pretty women, isn't it?

Growing up, I was faced with a dichotomy regarding my father. On the one hand, I looked askance at him as an insufferable egoist, while on the other hand, he was my strong, handsome, intelligent benefactor. He was very proud of me, so I became Daddy's girl. He championed my singing talent, and he loved to show me off to his friends. However, rather than feeling empowered, I was often annoyed at his obvious ploy to get attention for himself. He'd ask me to sing as he awkwardly strummed his new electric guitar to accompany me.

Once, I let him accompany me at a high school event honoring our football team where I was asked to perform. For some (Freudian) reason, I positioned him out of sight behind the curtain onstage while I sang "My Heart Belongs to Daddy." Everyone thought I was singing to Mike, whose wife had just had a baby, and I was given a standing ovation. When my dad came bounding out from behind the curtain, I begrudgingly introduced him as the reason for my song.

I believe my ambivalence toward him was set in concrete when he came home from a party once without my mother, just to practice his guitar with my singing. When I asked him where Mom was, he told me he'd left her on the sidewalk outside the nightclub and had sped away to come home and be with me. He was so cavalier about it. I felt a deep sadness for my mother.

PING! I had just brought someone from Marin to San Francisco around 6:30 p.m. when a call came in to pick someone up from a bar on Castro Street. Stopping at the appointed corner, I watched a man and a woman head toward me from across the street. They were holding hands and laughing gaily. He was a tall, confident, and very straight-looking white bespectacled businessman of about forty-five, and she was a stunning black woman around thirty, shapely and well dressed. They whispered and laughed throughout their ride to the hotel. When I asked them where they were from, they mentioned that they were both doctors from different parts of the country attending a physicians' convention. In their private conversation, I overheard them talk briefly about their respective spouses. When I let them off at the Mark Hopkins Hotel, he put his arm around her and kissed her as they walked into the hotel.

I guess "What happens in San Francisco, stays in San Francisco" except when people like me write a book about it (smile). My apologies if you are married to a guy who frequents out of town conventions, for injecting possible suspicions about his behavior on such occasions.

When I was fifteen, Dad got me a job as a nurse's aide at the Presbyterian Hospital in Whittier. I felt a discernable resentment coming from the other nurse's aides, who regarded their job as a career, not a temporary job handed to them by an influential father. Still, I had some very memorable experiences there. One time, I was chased around the room by a guy I had just finished bed bathing. Turns out he was only there for tests and wasn't sick at all. Another time, I was looking after a woman named Rosemary, who was a habitual and unsuccessful suicide patient. She came in twice during my tenure there: once for jumping in an empty pool and once for slashing her wrists. She even had previous scars on her wrists. Every time she was wheeled into the hospital, there would be a palpable sigh among the staff. "Here comes Rosemary again!" This was her home away from home. I liked her and enjoyed visiting with her. She was glamorous and sophisticated. (How interesting that I was drawn to this ultimate victim, which I would later become, almost to the point of suicide myself).

She'd taken a liking to me after I had confided in her about my singing and handed her a 45-rpm demo record. I was excited when she decided to promote me to her contacts in the music business. Nothing much came of them, as they were local and relatively insignificant and were really interested in only one thing, which, thankfully, they never got. Luckily for me, one had a recording studio, which afforded me a few more single demo records for my collection and a lot of practice time with a mic.

When I was sixteen, Dad again took on a new passion: buying newer and bigger boats every year. His need to impress was insatiable, and he soon acquired a mooring in Long Beach and one in Avalon, along with an apartment in Avalon. He eventually became the commodore of the Catalina Yacht Club, and I began to enjoy becoming an island fixture every summer. I strutted around in my newly formed voluptuous body with my cocoa-buttered tan and my sexy (1957-style) one-piece bathing suit. I also enjoyed singing from time to time at various clubs in Avalon. For seven years, we took our newest "stink-pot" (motor boat) to Avalon and lived in our apartment there every summer.

At seventeen, I boasted about having three dates a night in Avalon, even though I was still a virgin. My Jezebel was in full bloom. I was not going to let any guy be with me long enough to become his victim like my mother, who suffered so much being married to my dad.

As more threads unravel and dots are connected, I'm now aware that my "Jezebel" trait first revealed itself when I was in eighth grade.

I had two girlfriends, Suzanne and Janet, who walked home from school with me every day, along with a boy named John. One day, John informed us that he was going to ask one of us to go steady. He would pick one girl every day to finish the walk with. On the second or third time he picked me, he blurted out that he had something he wanted to ask me. I knew immediately what he was going to say, and I picked up speed and then ran away from him as fast as I could. He yelled, "Wait! I want to ask you to go steady with me!" I turned and stuck my tongue out at him and continued running home to plop on my bed and cry into my pillow.

In high school, I lucked out and went with the dreamiest guy on the football team, Ronnie, who had wavy blond hair and sexy brown eyes. Things were going along great until one day; I heard that some-one caught him in the boys' locker room posing in front of a mirror, flexing his muscles. Ah-hah! Now I had him. I couldn't wait to exer-cise my feminine power and demean him by saying, "Hi, muscle man!" Things never were so great after that: I was thrown over by a cute blond, brown-eyed cheerleader (whom he later married).

Later, I dated Bill, another guy on the football team. I enjoyed being his girlfriend and hanging with the "in" crowd, but when he asked me to go steady and gave me his letterman's sweater and class ring to wear around my neck, I was not thrilled. I wore them for about a week, and then I couldn't stand it any longer and gave him back his sweater and ring. I felt like I had released a heavy ball and chain from around my neck. Everyone sided with Bill, the football hero, which took me down a few notches in popularity. I did essentially the same thing to my boyfriend Pete at Cal Berkeley when he wanted to pin me. But this time, instead of giving in to him for a minute, I ran out of his frat house late at night and bolted home before he could finish his sentence. That was the end of Pete and me. And so it went ad infini-tum until I was twenty-two. If I didn't run, I would find a way to insult them so they would run from me if they got too close.

PING! A rider called Fred stood waiting for me on the corner of Union and Divisadero as I was on my way home to Novato in Marin. He was also headed in that direction. He was a portly seventy-year-old man who had a hangdog expression of perpetual sadness. With feigned joviality, he announced, "Hi, I'm Fred, but you can call me Freddy!" I told him he reminded me of my old college boyfriend Pete at UC Cal. That seemed to please him, and then he added, "I used to know a guy name Pete at Cal. What year were you there?" (Before you jump to conclusions, it was not the same year, so it was not the same Pete.) We continued our conversation about our university days. He said he was in a thirty-five-year marriage and had three grown children. But his most poignant admission was regarding what he believed to be the love of his life at Cal. He recalled how they used to drive to the hills above the campus and lie on the grass looking up at the stars, talking about the future. But on the day he proposed to her, she mysteriously turned cold and walked away. She never answered any of his calls and avoided him on campus whenever their paths crossed. He never knew why she did that. He said it took him twelve years to get over his grief before he met his present wife. With a hint of sadness, he said he would never forget her. I couldn't breathe. I remained silent the rest of the trip.

I fell into what I would call the "dishonorable tradition" of rushing sororities and became a ZTA at Cal. Although all the more "classy" sororities had rejected me, I found that my sisters at ZTA were a lot like me. We were a rebellious group of "unclassy" (not from established old money) women with diverse talents and backgrounds. However, the next semester I discovered that a particular diversity was definitely not encouraged when I was on the other side of the rush culture. To prepare for the upcoming rush week, our house mother admonished us against accepting anyone of color, Asian, Latino, or Jewish heritage. I was inherently repulsed by this but brushed it aside and went along for the ride. I am ashamed when I remember this incident, but it seems we now belong to a culture that does exactly the same thing: brush our morals aside when it's expedient to do so. This may have played a part in blocking my path to self-love. It is now my firm belief that personal integrity is one of the major keys to self-love. How many times have I gone along with the crowd, muzzling that quiet, still voice inside my head?

3

THAT OLD BLACK MAGIC
Blinds Me with Love

When I turned twenty-two, there was one guy who managed to penetrate my Jezebel firewall—my Catalina Island lover. He was the most astonishingly handsome and intriguing man I'd ever met. His irresistible charm held me captive. Maybe it was his light green eyes that seemed to cross ever so slightly when looking deeply into mine, or his wide, welcoming smile suggesting a promise of something exciting later. Richard Gere in *Pretty Woman* comes to mind as a fairly accurate example of how I remembered him looking and being.

Or perhaps it just had to do with the fact that it was a summer romance on an island. By its very nature, it was inherently noncommittal and temporary. Perfect! But I was too smug. I was not prepared for what was about to unfold.

As a teenager, with television being in its black-and-white infancy and with only a weekly segment of *Hopalong Cassidy* to look forward to, I was addicted to reading the daily comics, especially the Sunday edition in full color. One in particular: *Brenda Starr* was about a glamorous redheaded newspaper reporter. The love of her life was a handsome mystery man called Basil St. John, who grew black orchids and who always appeared and then disappeared mysteriously. I will call my island lover Basil St. John, because he turned out to be both the love of my life and my mystery man, and instead of black orchids, he wove swirls of black magic around me like a spider web.

We began our affair on this island paradise where Basil was captain of his catamaran and a bartender at a restaurant called The Galleon. I first met him while sitting on the "pickup" wall that separated the beach from the main street. As I sat there demurely, watching all the cute guys pass by, he came right up to me with his melting vanilla ice cream cone, which, of course, dripped on my knee. Seizing the opportunity, he gave me a seductive look and asked, "May I?" Not waiting for an answer, he bent down to lick it off. Sometime during that summer, at the ripe old age of twenty-two, my life as a virgin came to a screeching halt.

It happened one night on Dad's boat. We had been salsa dancing at one of the island's backstreet nightclubs and ended up taking a shore boat to our boat. It was unoccupied and welcoming, since Dad was up at our apartment on the hill. Basil and I sat out on the back deck talking and making out until the wee hours. I had a sudden realization that everything was quiet, which meant that all the shore boats were probably done for the night. I frantically yelled, "Shore boat, shore boat!" while he remained quietly composed, waiting for me to calm down and relax into the inevitable.

Others had tried, but he alone succeeded on that starry night inside a boat that rocked gently with every wave we made. His kisses were so tender and passionate; I couldn't resist his wandering hands on my body. I groaned in ecstasy as I felt the sharp pain of my very first penetration. Holding me in his arms and kissing my forehead as he smoothed the hair back from my eyes, he asked, "Now that I have your body, how do I get inside your mind?"

PING! It was 5:30 p.m., and I had to shake off my agitated state of mind after having been delayed an hour due to a misdirected pickup for my supplements before I startedy Uber run for the day. I then repeated my mantra and told God that I trusted it was all

perfect. My Uber app directed me to a marina in San Rafael where a man named Mark requested a ride.

A ruggedly handsome, swashbuckling man approached my car and greeted me with bright enthusiasm, which did not match my mood. He asked how I was, and I replied, "A little short of fantastic, but there's hope."

Smiling, he said, "Hope is the most important thing there is. Without it there's nothing. But it's best not to have expectations."

I surmised, "You sound like a philosopher." There was an immediate connection between us, and we began a conversation that exploded with energy and excitement.

I looked through the rearview mirror at his face while he talked and was intrigued by his expressive eyebrows and sparkling blue eyes. He was so good looking, I wondered if he was in the movie business. It turned out he was a computer tech for most of the big movie studios in Hollywood.

When I asked him where he lived, he told me he had many houses in the US and in Costa Rica. He lived on his 48' Chris Craft boat whenever he stayed in Marin. He was a young-looking fifty with two kids, a three-year-old and a five-year-old. His girlfriend lived in Marin. He admitted he was basically a wanderer. I wondered how many hearts he had broken in his wanderlust life.

On top of everything else, he owned thirty-five different vehicles, including antique cars, motorcycles, jeeps, luxury cars, and a couple of yachts. I said that he sounded like a mini Jay Leno, and he responded by telling me that they were actually good friends. I thought to myself, *OMG, this man is the ultimate catch!* (If he were indeed "catchable.") But he really capped it off when he told me he had studied and read the whole *A Course in Miracles* twice with his mother. Despite his many personal modes of transportation, he mentioned he was a chronic user of

Ubers wherever he went, often using them five or six times a day for various odd jobs.

I said, "Well, you are the perfect advertisement for Uber." He agreed. We ended the trip with a warm handshake and an eye-to-eye acknowledgment. As I drove off, I thanked God for having made me late so I could experience meeting this truly amazing man. Like so many men I have fallen for in the past, he was a gentle reminder that such men very seldom choose to commit to a long-term relationship.

Thus began my fifteen-year obsession of unrequited love with my mystery man. That summer, I spent many evenings sitting at The Galleon bar flirting with him and playing the role of a femme fatale. After two or more Vodka Collins, I sang Black Magic to him and later recorded it for him to keep. I transferred to UCLA partly because of him and partly for the great art and theater courses that were offered there.

He lived in a big house right on the beach in Venice with a group of his wild, openly sexual friends. They were all older and far more sophisticated than I. We reenacted our Catalina tryst many times upstairs in his spacious bedroom. He gave me a gold bracelet with my initials engraved on a perfume container charm and said he wouldn't mind if that was all I wore for the rest of the day. He thought I looked better naked than clothed. Once we took a small outboard motor boat to Catalina, just the two of us facing twenty-two miles of ocean alone together in what was little more than a dinghy. I had no fear because I was with HIM. I savored each moment, submerged in the thrill of my desire for him, which was embellished by the salty smell of the sea and the wind whipping through my clothes and ruffling my hair.

I loved the feel of his warm, smooth skin and strong muscles and his light green eyes that penetrated my soul. He often teased me by sucking my lips between his teeth, and then he'd suddenly let go as if to say he had to stop himself before he swallowed me whole.

We often finished each other's sentences, but he never said, "I love you." He only managed to say, "Lose ten pounds and I might fall in love with you." My lover, my abuser—and now I know what it's like to be under that spell.

Later, when I heard the news from a friend of his that he'd married someone in the family way, I took off my bracelet and threw it in the ocean. My spirit was broken. I no longer had the desire to continue my studies at UCLA, so I quit in my senior year. I brought down the curtain on Catalina and Basil St. John and walked barefoot into my next scenery change—Hollywood.

4

LET ME ENTERTAIN YOU
Pleeeze?!

Having Basil still on my mind led me to desperate acts of defiance, and what better place than Hollywood to do the deed? Looking hot in my sixties mini dresses with my knee-high boots, I sought my revenge through fame and fortune. I sashayed in and out of agents' and directors' offices with backroom couches that promised stardom. But stardom never came. You can imagine what "came" instead. Being raised by an openly lascivious father, I was never surprised or insulted by the animal nature of men in power. And I was equally complicit with my agenda to become a star by any means necessary. Funny how the "whatever means possible" never panned out.

One of the things that came instead was Basil St. John, not yet divorced but in and out of my life like a rented car. I couldn't resist. My justifiable anger was reduced to pitiful slave-like acquiescence. He'd show up in the middle of the night wherever I happened to be living. We'd spend one or two days of nonstop bliss (or was it agony?) together, and then he would disappear for another six to twelve months. I was hypnotized by this wild, unpredictable man and never stopped thinking about him. He certainly knew how to play the game to keep me permanently obsessed. Just like Brenda Starr, I was single and in love with a man who would never commit his love to me and who would always exit stage right . . . or was it left? I guess whichever way was quicker and more accessible.

In between sudden Basil St. John appearances, I turned my focus onto becoming a singing and acting star. I rented an apartment with my old college roommate Judee, who had graduated while I dropped out in my senior year. We lived down the street from the Whisky a Go Go on Sunset Blvd. I watched her star rise and shine as she gained regular TV appearances on *My Three Sons*, *Dr. Kildare*, and *Bonanza*. Meanwhile, I worked in an aluminum extrusion company taking orders. But stardom was always just a breath away. Trouble was, I could never quite catch my breath while jumping in and out of one bed of promises after another. Judee never had to stoop so low. She had some sort of magic gismo, (called self-love) which I frantically tried to find but never could. I did manage to have professional pictures taken for my nonexistent resume, which boosted my ego if nothing else.

Not to be outdone, I discovered my own magic formula that brought me another kind of ego gratification. It was a bit of a distraction, but I didn't lack for attention and fun when I became friends with a group of prominent European men, a couple of whom lived temporarily in our apartment complex. One was Francois, a very sweet, soft-spoken Frenchman and a foreign car salesman, who looked a little like Charlie Chaplin. There was Vittorio, or "Vitto," a tall, young, muscular Italian ballet dancer in Vegas, somewhat like Rudolph Nureyev; Gregorio, a slightly bald Italian and an importer of Italian knits; Serge, an Armenian architect with curly gray hair and a superbly tanned face, looking like "The Most Interesting Man in the World." He designed famous nightclubs and restaurants in Hollywood. Giorgio, with his boyish good looks, was an Italian Blue Angel pilot, and Raoul, a tall, bald, portly Frenchman, was the owner of an art gallery on Sunset Strip.

They adopted me as their communal female playmate and included me in many of their soirees and evenings at fancy nightclubs and restaurants in Hollywood. I knew a little Italian and much more French and was able to join in their discussions over coffee at our favorite street café on Sunset Boulevard. Also, Serge had a fabulous apartment above the Millionaire's Club on La Cienega, the hottest new nightclub at that time, which he had designed. He often cooked dinner for us, displaying his expertise as a chef of French and Armenian food. Once, he invited Mickey Rooney to dinner, and we all enjoyed the many Hollywood stories Mickey told.

Another time, Serge brought out his collection of belly dance costumes and Moroccan kaftans, which we wore as we danced seductively around his apartment to the sensuous drumbeat of Middle Eastern LPs (long playing vinyl records).

PING! A call came in to go to the Buck Institute in Novato. There stood three well-dressed men of East Indian origin, all laughing as I pulled up to the front entrance. The tallest one, named Sanjit, sat in the front seat with me, and I asked him to tell me about the Buck Institute, since I didn't know what it was for. I had always wondered about the stark white, ultra-modern building situated among dark green oak trees high on a hill facing the 101. It looked very stately and important. He said it was an anti-aging institute and that all three of them were each around 120 years old. They all laughed when I looked at them in disbelief.

I found out they were highly regarded doctors who specialized in preventative medicine. They had come to Buck to learn life-saving scientific methods for reversing Alzheimer's. They informed me that they were British Indian Bengalis who also worked for the BBC to promote well-being. We related on so many other issues that I felt an immediate connection with them. I told them I felt like they were my "soul brothers" and that I would include them in my book. This pleased them so much they insisted on taking a selfie with me when we arrived in Sausalito. This ride was the highlight of my day and week.

Once when I was out of work for two weeks and my food and money were running out, Francois dropped by and handed me three boxes of spaghetti to tide me over. Finally, a week later, I found work in a doctor's office and excitedly went out and bought a lamb chop and frozen peas. Just as I sat down to eat, Serge called and invited me to his place for a small dinner party. I let loose some loud expletives at his terrible timing and not so politely declined his invitation. He forgave me later, and we made up with a delicious private home-cooked meal by Serge and a few kisses from me.

One time a big group of us drove down to Riverside in separate cars to watch the car races. After the races, we went out to dinner and got ripping drunk. We ended up forming a parade down the middle of the street. Everyone pretended to play some loud instrument while they pushed me in a grocery cart as their reigning queen. At the last restaurant, they kicked us out because Vitto decided to dance on the tables. I thought he was spectacular! Later that night I had at least three visitors in my hotel room, one after the other. What was unique about this experience as they took turns making love to me was the sweet way they each asked my permission. I guess they felt that our friendship was more important. This probably covered over any feelings of guilt or self-loathing I may have had. After all, they couldn't help it: they were men!

In every situation, including this, I was almost always in a haze of intoxication. Nothing I said or did had any substance or moral relevancy. I was like a rag doll being tossed from one scene to another without a backbone of true self-worth. My life was just a series of momentary flashes of ego gratification. I can only thank God that drugs were not part of the scene in those days or I might have been a goner. I was not an alcoholic, just a social drunk and an embarrassment to myself.

5

WHAT'S LOVE GOT TO DO WITH IT?

Absolutely Nothing!

PING! I pulled up to a mobile home and Doris, a woman in her fifties who looked a little bit like the forties movie icon Jean Harlow, climbed into the back seat. Her platinum blond hair in a shoulder-length bob and her retro sundress even reminded me of the fifties. The first words out of her mouth were "Fuck . . . I left my wallet in the house. . . . Wait, I'll be right back." When she returned, she was petulant and seemed to be preoccupied with something. Then suddenly, she yelled, "Fuck it, I'm late! Can you please hurry? I'll miss my appointment."

Right after that she sighed, saying, "I'm sorry. Don't pay any attention to me. I'm just getting over a relationship and everything is just crazy right now." She told me the story about her latest love affair with a "lyin', cheatin' SOB" who dumped her for a younger woman. She said he was no prize himself, referring to his age, which was at least ten years older than she was. She confided in me that he had made her his sex slave and would appear on her doorstep for a "booty call" whenever he felt like it. She knew it was demeaning and wrong, but he excited her, and she didn't know how to say "no" to him.

Last night, she finally came to her senses when he didn't show up for a dinner date, telling her later that he was embarrassed to be seen with an old hag like her. I gave her my ten cents' worth, saying, "You could do a hell of a lot better than him. The truth is, he doesn't deserve to be seen with a beautiful, classy woman like you."

I sneaked a peek at her in my rearview mirror, and I noticed her eyes were beginning to well up. She looked back at me and smiled, whispering, "Thank you." I turned on the radio and asked what kind of music she liked. "Oh, it doesn't matter. Play whatever you want," she replied. So I put in a little mood-changing music with "Girls Just Wanna Have Fun." The rest of the ride was rockin', and we arrived right on time. My passenger had become transformed, compliments of Cindy Lauper.

Moving on to one of the lowest points of my life, which I had conveniently forgotten until I wrote down her awful story: I remember being in a coffee shop on Melrose after auditioning for a play when I noticed one of the other actors giving me the once-over. He ambled over to my table and asked if he could join me. When he said he saw something in me that screamed "star material," that got my attention. I let down my guard and said, "Sure." From there, he held me captive for a solid seven hours, convincing me that he had the means to make a star out of me, if I would just put my trust in him completely and swear my allegiance to him. He asserted that he was the Welsh stepbrother of Richard Burton, who was then married to Elizabeth Taylor. He had beady black eyes and crooked teeth, and he didn't have a car. God knows why I didn't see the red flags waving furiously in front of my eyes. He was a hypnotist and a con man, whom I will call Rasputin.

We moved into a musty old castle in Hollywood Hills owned by an older, wealthy woman acquaintance of his. We stayed on the top floor. It turned out that he was a sadomasochist who would whip me with a belt every night "to bring out the charismatic, vulnerable sexiness hiding within." He thought he could make me into another Marilyn

Monroe. After each whipping, he would either have me walk back and forth in my underwear to see if I had any charisma yet, or he would tie me to the bedposts and rape me. I don't remember the whipping ever hurting that much. If it did, I must have felt I deserved it: my penance for being such a wicked woman. It may have been just a symbolic whipping to humiliate me, anchoring his dominance over me.

In my demented state of mind, by this time, the rape was exciting and sexually fulfilling. I let myself go completely because of my emotional detachment from this man. He meant nothing to me except perhaps a ticket to stardom. How cynical is that? Had I really sunk that low? I let him do things to me I'd never let anyone else do, and I screamed with orgasmic pleasure each time. I felt like I had some kind of power over him with my feminine submissiveness. And, of course, I was subconsciously playing him to become the star he envisioned me to be. This part of my life has been hidden in the back pages of my brain, and I only just regained my memory of it after writing Doris's story.

As if this weren't enough, I learned that Rasputin was married and had a two-year-old baby. He ordered me to use my dad's credit card to pay their rent and food when I drove him to their house once a week. To illustrate how devious he was and how conveniently stupid I was, he talked me into letting him play my part in a movie. I won a part in the movie called *The Courtship of Eddie's Father* playing an artist at a concession where I sold handmade ties with sexy women painted on them. I actually painted all the ties previously, but he sat in the chair I was supposed to sit in while the star came and purchased one of the ties. I don't remember what my payoff was for that. I guess it was confirmation of my total lack of self-worth.

I soon got tired of him and his twenty-four seven BS and made my first rational decision: to move out. I found a room available above the Sunset Strip with an actress friend of mine. But he was not to be deterred. He started coming around and once again worked his "bad" black magic on me by dangling the mention of a project he was working on, which looked "promising for my career."

This hypnotic fast-talker fooled not only me but also a whole host of people in Hollywood. He managed to charm a UHS TV station to give him his own show (free of charge), and he enlisted some reputable, but out of work, TV directors and actors into creating a weekly drama series. I, of course, starred in the first drama, Chekhov's *The Boor*. The leading man, Frank de Kova, a well-known character movie actor who played Indian chiefs, came in drunk on the day of the shoot and was fired. Rasputin, who was the director, took over his role, reading the script below the camera line of vision.

Time after time he gave me the wrong cue and I had to improvise. In the end I received a standing ovation. Something had taken over my conscious mind, and I was transformed. I had become the embodiment of Greta Garbo as a tormented woman throughout the whole show, and nothing could take me out of character.

I'm ashamed to say I participated in a scheme of Rasputin's to enlist "wannabe" actors and actresses to pay money to act in our TV shows. But after *The Boor*, we struggled to put another show together. There were many roadblocks, and people began to question Rasputin's authority. He became intolerable, growing more demanding and more dependent on me every day. He was a pervasive presence in my life, and he clung to me like a leech with his constant stream of lies and demands.

Our last relevant time together was on a road trip to Big Sur, and I just couldn't take it anymore. In the middle of a screaming match, I stopped the car on that dangerous, narrow road high above the ocean and told him to get out. Actually, I pushed him until he was out and then shut the door and sped off. In my rearview mirror I saw him stand there, watching in disbelief as I drove away. Thirty minutes later, I came to my senses, feeling guilty. I made a U-turn and found him walking along the road. I picked him up, and we didn't speak a word the whole way home.

That same week, the TV show was canceled and Rasputin was found out for who he wasn't. He disappeared from all of our lives like a puff of exhaust fumes, leaving toxic residue on our bruised psyches. I don't remember if we paid back all the money we took from the "wannabes." I think we tried our best. I do know no one sued us or took us to court.

Between Basil and Rasputin, my self-worth was degraded, and my youthful innocence had been totally corrupted. Not liking myself very much made it difficult to relate to people in a warm and friendly way. I kept getting into circumstances where I would continually give my power away, believing everyone was smarter and more worthy than I. Although I was developing a well of emotions to draw from for acting, in real life it did little to bring about success or happiness. I was unaware that life was teaching me some important lessons at this point. I was just a victim of circumstances and did not have the power or the will to understand or change anything.

PING! Uber sent me to a home in Tiburon where a short, very stocky man with a full head of curly black hair came out the front door and waved at me as he headed toward the car. He looked comical as he struggled to pick up speed with his short, fat legs while pulling a large piece of luggage behind him. He finally made it to the car, and I opened the trunk and helped him lift the bag up and in. Wiping the sweat from his brow, he smiled and thanked me. Breathing rather heavily, he managed to stuff himself into the back seat of my car as I pulled the front passenger seat up to give him more room. I asked if he wanted a bottle of water, which I kept on hand for long-distance riders. He accepted it gratefully. He said his name was Andy and he was a standup comedian and had a gig in San Diego that weekend. He reminded me so much of someone I had known a long time ago, another actor/comedian.

Suddenly he contorted his face into a pout and messed up his hair, imitating a well-known celebrity called Donald Trump. "I'll tell you a really YUGE secret. When I'm President of the United States, I'm going to cover the White House with gold leaf. Then I'll feel comfortable living in it." He cracked up at his own joke and said he just thought of it. "Maybe I'll use that tomorrow night."

I cracked up too but then added, "It would be no joke if he actually did become president."

We both became morbidly silent for a good five minutes, and then he said, "Moving on, seen any good movies lately?"

I welcomed his change of subject and said, "No, I'm too busy living my own movie." He liked that. We chatted amicably all the way to the airport, and it felt like I had known him from another lifetime. We shook hands, and he with his short legs and stubby fingers toting a large suitcase disappeared into the terminal as another call came in.

Shortly after Rasputin exited stage left, a big, sweet, chubby, middle-aged character actor named Stanley, who was part of the TV team, took a liking to me. He drove an MG sports car, which made him look kind of ridiculous with his big frame stuffed into such a small space. (Yes, this was the man Andy reminded me of.) He liked to make me laugh with his many character impersonations, and we enjoyed each other's company. Soon we became lovers, and he made me his mistress. The tables had turned; instead of me supporting a married man *and* his wife *and* child, now a married man was supporting me.

This arrangement didn't last long, because he walked into my apartment one day unannounced while I was rehearsing a love scene in a play for which a friend and I were auditioning. We all looked at each other, shocked. My friend had no idea I had a lover who had a key, my lover didn't know I was rehearsing a scene from a play, and I wasn't expecting him to show up in the middle of the afternoon when I would normally be attending classes at UCLA. His unannounced visitation marked the official end of that affair since he didn't believe me. I was a better actor than I thought as far as the love scene was concerned, but apparently a lousy actor when it came to trying to convince him I was just acting.

So much for my dreams of love and/or stardom, but I still didn't get it. These star-studded illusions, called "opportunities," continued to tempt me at every turn, looking completely new and different and more promising each time. But it was always the same song trying to tell me that it had nothing to do with love or my soul's purpose. Doggedly, I put another nickel in and played it over and over and over again.

6

STRAWBERRY FIELDS FOREVER
Adventures in Alternate Realities

Bouncing around from one apartment dwelling to another, each one visited at least once by Basil, I came in contact with a woman named Patti at a cocktail bar on the strip. She took a liking to me, and I was flattered, as she was a striking, tall blond with a strong sense of self. We became close friends, nightclubbing together at various clubs on the strip, and one day, she introduced me to her boyfriend, Richard, who also took a liking to me. In retrospect, he was much like a tall, lanky Humphrey Bogart, and she was very much like Lauren Bacall. That resemblance never occurred to me until now.

They offered to give me a permanent place to live in their beautiful modern redwood-and-glass house in the Hollywood Hills. During this time, I became Patti's lap dog. I believed everything she said and admired everything she did. I followed her around like a puppy. Although her strong, outgoing personality gave one the impression she was in charge, in reality Dick held sway over her because of her financial dependency and because she was deeply in love with him and so afraid of losing him. He loved her but had a nonchalant attitude toward her and basically toward everything (like Bogart). Often she would call him on his insensitivity, and he would just look at her and then begin laughing as he pulled her into him and kissed her passionately, shutting down any meaningful dialogue they could have had.

I enjoyed their friendship. It afforded me a (false) feeling of security and groundedness that had been so lacking in my "flying by the seat of my pants" life. For the first time, I felt like I was not alone but had the support of two mature, intelligent people. In retrospect, I think he was a father figure to me, and she was like my big sister.

Little did I know I was about to be indoctrinated into the world of LSD. However, I was not interested in having any, as I feared losing control of my already fragile mind. So they asked me to hang around at every weekend LSD party to make sure nobody jumped off the balcony. Richard was a habitual pothead, smoking almost every day. But he kept his wits about him, as he was a real estate broker who made good money to support his wealthy lifestyle. One day, I experimented with pot while painting a life-sized, full-figured self-portrait, which turned out so well that he paid me $200 for it, which was a lot in those days. It took me all of four hours to draw and do an impressionistic rendering in acrylics. The picture featured me slouched in a chair in my panties. My shirt was loosely unbuttoned, exposing one breast. That was a pretty good representation of where I was at in my life.

Finally, after a year, I surrendered to the LSD temptress. Patti and Dick abstained so they could monitor me and allow me to feel completely safe while I went on my trip. Nothing frightening happened; I was just completely immobilized as I watched a kaleidoscopic show of sparkling colors. My spiritual takeaway involved seeing myself in a flowing dress of rainbow colors, floating down a giant staircase. I had a clear realization that this represented my very essence as a multifaceted artist descending from heavenly realms and merging with earthly me.

Coming off the trip, we went to Denny's for a snack around 2 a.m. A couple in the next booth was in the midst of an argument. Their heads began growing like big red balloons. Their eyes bulged out and their tongues wagged through bared teeth while their necks grew long and skinny, balancing their huge balloon heads. At the same time, another cartoon couple walked past our booth, looking a lot like Frankenstein walking stiffly beside a gal with foot-long eyelashes. I stifled a mega-decibel laugh so as not to draw attention to my chemical high.

PING! After a five-minute wait and no response to my call, a woman finally appeared. She walked slowly toward the car and barely acknowledged that she was Pauline, the one who'd called. As we drove to Petaluma, I noticed that she reeked of whiskey. She seemed very sweet but disoriented as she rambled on incoherently about nothing in particular. Her energy was extremely low as she slumped against the corner of the car.

I tried to bring up subjects that she might be interested in, but nothing seemed to stick. From my rearview mirror, I spotted a perpetually worried look. She admitted that she had been drinking and was embarrassed. Finally, she told me about her big problem involving a guy she couldn't get rid of who had been living in her house for years. She recounted the times she'd tried and how he'd twisted her efforts against her and had threatened to call the police on her.

Her story made the hairs on the back of my neck stand on end; I couldn't resist. In a firm voice, I said, "Pauline, you need to take back your power. Did you know your drinking is robbing you of your power?"

She sat quietly for about five minutes and, upon reflection, replied, "That is really good advice. Thank you. I will do that." As she opened the door to leave, the color had returned to her cheeks. Her eyes were brighter and I caught a glimpse of a smile on her face. I reminded her that she had to stand up for herself and that she had every right to call the police and have him evicted. She thanked me again, and I couldn't believe how quickly she had seemingly

transformed. It was obvious she was ready to hear those words to finally change the trajectory of her life. Her spirit recognized the truth and came alive. Of course I have no idea if it actually did change her life. Perhaps it was a good start in that direction.

As I drove away, I began to realize how important this Uber job is. I am like a social worker on wheels, and my passengers are also my teachers. There was no agenda or plan on my part to counsel this woman. The experience happened organically and spontaneously. The words issued forth unexpectedly, much like the time I yelled, "I can't be anything to anyone until I love myself" to my grandmother. What I told this woman I was also saying to myself. It came from the very depths of my being. Somehow her story reminded me of Rasputin, when I also needed to learn to stand in my power. That is why I recite my intentional prayer every day before Uber driving. This practice effectively sets aside the ego, which allows Spirit to do the work through me to reveal the truth and to heal a situation.

Among all the memories of my time with Patti and Dick, one of the most memorable involved the night Patti and I went to a club in Ventura. We were sitting at the piano bar listening to Bobby Troop when she suddenly disappeared. An hour later she returned and told me she'd met Jonathan Winters, the top standup comedian of that time. Patti had engaged him in a conversation in which she'd pretended they'd met before at a "make-believe" party. Then she talked Jonathan and the Bobby Troop trio into following us back to our house after the bar closed. They stayed until dawn, with Jonathan recounting the amazing stories of the time he'd had a mental breakdown and what he'd experienced while in custody.

As the story goes, "In 1959, comedian Jonathan Winters reputedly climbed into the *Balclutha*'s rigging (in SF harbor) and refused to come down, shouting to the police gathered below: 'Where am I from? I'm from outer space, man, outer space. I'm the man in the moon. I'm John Q. What's it to you?' Winters was eventually captured;

as he was dragged off the boat, he yelled 'this boat is a fake, it's got an outboard motor on it.'"*

*Digital Archive at Found SF.

Jonathan recounted the whole story in his own words and added the fact that he was also "butt naked." He said they put him in a straitjacket and locked him up in jail. He was later transferred to a convalescent home, where many confrontations with fellow inmates and orderlies ensued. He entertained us with poignantly hilarious stories for hours.

Finally, the day came when Patti and Dick decided to move to Vegas. I felt like the rug had been pulled out from under me. I didn't realize, until then, how dependent I had become on their friendship. They were the center of my world.

Although we visited each other a few times in Vegas and at my new apartment in Hollywood, I became a Buddhist to fill the hole they left in my heart, so I was no longer available to them. My time and energy now revolved around my new Buddhist practice instead of around Patti and Dick.

Basil also lived in Vegas, and I called him up once from Dick and Patti's house, and Dick took it upon himself to listen in on my conversation from another room. This was very distracting, because I could hear his breathing and clicking tongue after some of my apparent faux pas. Dick was concerned that I was being a pushover and tried to coach me, but I was humiliated and angry and unreceptive to his suggestions. I probably should have listened.

In retrospect, the person I was during my time with Patti and Dick is repugnant to me. I was the perfect lapdog girlfriend to Patti. I guess that comes with having zero self-worth. We kept in touch from time to time, and ten years later, she invited me to her new home in Ojai after her marriage and subsequent divorce from Dick. It was a real eye-opener when I found that another obsequious lapdog girlfriend had replaced me. It was like watching a movie of how I used to be with her. How often do we get a chance to see a reenactment of our life?

During the editing process of this book, I hunted down my old friend Dick who is now eighty-seven and living in Florida. He filled in some blanks for me and confessed he had been a real jerk to Patti, who died seven years ago of emphysema. She actually died of a broken heart, because he had cheated on her during their marriage, and she had a nervous breakdown and was hospitalized. According to Dick, after their divorce she associated with a group of lesbians and never had another boyfriend and never got married again. Dick told me that he, on the other hand, has led a charmed life with another woman, his second wife of twenty-four years. We ask ourselves, where's the justice? This story may be all too common among women who "love too much." Patti demonstrates the very real danger to our psyche when we abdicate our personal power so completely to another. Her attachment was like dead weight around his neck, and her expectations brought nothing but disappointment and ruin. I felt so sorry for this woman who I thought had such great potential. But isn't it interesting that I was to Patti what she was to Dick?

I WILL SURVIVE

Goddammit!

P ING! A call from a woman named Elizabeth had me pull up to a tall young woman who stoically stood like a statue with a far-away look in her eyes and her long chestnut colored hair blowing across her face. She didn't move for a full minute until I beeped my horn. She suddenly came alive and nodded apologetically upon entering my car. Brushing her hair aside, I noticed her mascara was smeared. She pulled out her compact and quickly dabbed her eyes with a Kleenex and proceeded to powder her nose. After applying fresh makeup, she sat back with a sigh, ready to take on the day. But her shoulders started to shake as she broke down in tears again. After a while, I asked if she'd like to talk about it. She looked up at me through my rearview mirror and took a moment to contemplate whether or not to trust a complete stranger with her story. (I wanted to tell her that what happens in an Uber, stays in an Uber.)

Slowly she found the words: "He's fucking married to a GUY!" That brought a torrent of uncontrollable sobs. In between sobs her squeaky voice attempted to tell the sordid details of their affair. "I knew he was married, but he swore he loved me and promised he would divorce her. But it turns out she was a he, and he had no intention of ending his marriage to HIM! I don't get it. I just don't get it!"

I had nothing to say, so I let her cry her heart out for the rest of the blessedly short trip. When we got to her destination, I reached around and looked her squarely in the eyes and said, "You are a very beautiful woman who deserves to be loved by a great guy. He'll probably come when you least expect it. Be open and ready for that. Don't let your broken heart block your chances for loving again. OK?" She took a deep breath and thanked me as she opened the door. She hurried off and then turned for a brief moment to give me a grateful nod.

Deep in debt and feeling increasingly unworthy of love, I traded my Ford Mustang in for a cheaper Ford Pinto to take me to the next stage of my life—a theater in the round where I played a bit part and inadvertently fell in love with the star. I'll call him Nameless the Clown, who, in real life, was a married man. He later became a "second banana" comedian on a famous TV show that lasted ten years and later starred in a classic comedy movie. He was very tall, with penetrating blue eyes. He had the look of someone who secretly knew a hilarious joke and could barely keep from laughing out loud at the thought of it. He could never keep a straight face. His face was like a billboard for his emotions. We often slipped away during a break in rehearsals and made out in some dark corner backstage. I adored him and almost forgot about Basil.

Nameless gave me the impression that his marriage was of no consequence and that his plan was to divorce her. I believed him because we were so connected intellectually and emotionally; I couldn't imagine anyone else having such a close relationship with him (my naiveté knew no bounds). Then I found out from a friend that he was in therapy for being a borderline homosexual. His friend strongly suggested I stay away from him. This revelation hurt and confused me. But later it made sense since our sexual relations consisted of me going down on him, and only once did we actually have normal sex. I didn't mind because by now I was falling madly in love with him.

Here is a perfect example of completely ignoring any red flags when it suits your agenda. Love is not blind; it's the ego that tricks you into thinking you're in love.

He swore that he didn't love his wife and was going to leave her, but lo and behold, she became "mysteriously" pregnant with his first child. I couldn't believe it. As he held me in his arms and told me this, my anger came out in full force as I screamed for him to leave. I didn't see or hear from him for three or four months after that, and when he finally called, he angrily accused me of giving him VD (venereal disease), which could have infected his newborn baby. I frantically went out to prove he was wrong. Three doctors assured me I didn't have VD, but their report didn't change a thing. His mind was made up, and the curtain came down hard on this clown. Just like my passenger, I knew what it felt like to fall hard with your eyes wide shut. So much for my deep, intellectual connection.

Ever since my teenage years, I obsessed about guys who were popular and hard to get. Then the minute they became attracted to me, they became intolerable slobbering idiots in my mind, or I fell for them so hard they dumped me for being too needy. It's obvious to me now; I had abdicated my personal power with Nameless and became unattractively needy.

Basil was the only man who had ever broken through that barrier. But by now, Basil was also gone. So I inadvertently started dating married men, not knowing they were married at first, but continuing after finding out, because it assured me a certain level of safety. Even so, with Nameless, I was not safe. I hadn't planned on falling "in love" with him. When he phoned and called me a whore for endangering his firstborn, I came frighteningly close to suicide. Luckily, I chickened out and chose to bear the pain as only a grim-faced movie heroine would.

8

IF YOU COULD READ MY MIND
You Probably Need a Psychiatrist

PING! My Uber app signaled a pickup in Marin at an apartment complex. I felt mildly annoyed as I waited for what seemed like a long time for my new passenger to emerge. Finally, a golf cart drove up in which sat pretty, dark-haired Miranda, along with all her baggage (literally and figuratively).

For the next forty-five minutes while driving her to San Francisco Airport, my social and therapeutic skills were put to the test. Feeling completely safe with me, a stranger, she wailed all the way to the airport. Apparently, her mother and her mother's boyfriend had thrown her out. They told her they hated her and didn't want anything more to do with her. Their confrontation concerned a large sum of money she felt they owed her. This was way out of my field of expertise, so I let her wail on and on and just nodded my head.

During the course of her story, it became obvious that the boyfriend was protecting her mother's financial interests. I planted the possibility in her mind that perhaps her mother really loved her and didn't know how to express it in front of her partner. By the time we reached the airport, Miranda's sobs had stopped. She looked more clear and confident and thanked me for indulging her.

By age twenty-four, I was having affairs with one married man after another in Hollywood, some noteworthy, others happily forgotten. One such affair was with a sixty-five-year-old Russian prince, who gave me expensive dresses designed by his ex-wife to wear on a trip to New York. He wined and dined me in the top New York restaurants and took me to a fashion show hosted by his ex-wife. I was in the company of some well-known celebrities, political personalities, and other prominent people, which I calculated would bode well for my career. My payment involved sexual fealty in our hotel room every night. I tightly closed my eyes while being ravaged by this creepy old man. It turns out this creepy old man had ties with the Mafia.

My life was a total illusion. It was a movie I created based on self-loathing. I wandered in and out of my life, jostled around by circumstances seemingly beyond my control. But I wore my mantle of victimhood like a proud foot soldier going in the opposite direction.

I had another affair with a William Morris talent agent who was really nice and sincerely liked me and wanted me to succeed. He was not particularly attractive but well connected enough to be another presumed ticket to stardom. He took me to Las Vegas and introduced me to some of his clients, one being Harry James, a big band icon of the forties and fifties. I vaguely remember having consumed thirteen or fourteen Black Russians when Harry sat on the couch next to me to speak with his agent. During the ensuing conversation, my head swiveled back and forth between Harry on my left and the agent on my right. My brain swirled, and as fate would have it, I threw up all over Harry's white dinner jacket. I was so drunk I wasn't even embarrassed. I passed out on a chaise lounge by the pool after that.

Fortunately, my agent friend was very forgiving and gave me a chance to prove my singing talent to an associate higher up in the agency, at a nightclub in Santa Monica later that month. But my opportunistic plan backfired as I, once again, downed more drinks than I could count before going onstage. I ended up slaughtering the song. I saw the disappointment in his eyes as I sang my last off-key note. I never saw him again.

Another short-lived affair involved a TV news anchor who took me to meet the California state governor, Pat Brown (Jerry Brown's father), at a party in his mansion in LA. Another involved a famous Broadway musical composer who took me to a party at Peggy Lee's house, where she treated me to a private musical concert with my date accompanying her on the piano. Before this much-appreciated impromptu concert, I observed a gaggle of Hollywood's elite mixed with a few "has beens" and "wannabes" in the other room, one of which was a handsome young actor apparently with Peggy's *extremely* obese daughter. His opportunistic agenda was painfully obvious to me. Perhaps this was a subtle message from the universe?

One other memorable affair, which was ongoing for several months, involved the president of a major TV network in New York. He was a tall, distinguished man with gray hair and laughing eyes. Every time he came to LA, he would contact me, and we would go out to dinner, then straight to his hotel room at the Beverly Hills Hotel. His favorite sex act was to reverse roles; he would pretend to be a woman, and I would have to be the man ravaging him. One night, he handed me a reefer that was laced with something he called Acapulco Gold. The drug made me feel completely disconnected from reality. The best I can describe my experience is that it was like living in a memory that never happened. I flailed about and begged him to help me out of this surreal nightmare. He was very caring and held me until I came around. That was our last time together. He sent me a box full of vinyl record albums the following week as a thank you and farewell present.

After all these colorful alliances, not one paid off regarding my original intention—to move my singing and acting career forward. I was like a sleepwalker going through the motions of opportunistic indiscretion in which I drowned out the small, still voice in my head with sex, drugs, and alcohol. Did it ever occur to me that I was nothing more than a cheap whore? No, never!

Poor little drunkard: like a soggy ragdoll full of booze, not responsible for a single moment of her life. Her dress is torn and her button eyes are gone. What will become of her? Is she just a ghost in a wishing well?

ISN'T SHE LOVELY

A Gift for Another Mother

A mid these episodes in Hollywood, I had gone back to school to finish up my education at UCLA for a BA in fine arts. While attending my last semester there, I got pregnant by a friend who was a student set designer in the theater department. He wasn't married but confessed he was in love with someone else. At a loss as to what to do, I told my folks (they were both remarried). Dad demanded I bring him to his house for a talk. The poor guy nearly passed out when Dad forcefully told him that his only option was to marry me. I assured him that I thought otherwise.

I decided not to abort (as I had done before in a back alley and almost bled to death). I wanted to learn my lesson and never get pregnant again. I wanted to be like the brave character Leslie Caron played in *The L-Shaped Room*. So I rented a squalid apartment in Venice, California, with creaky, slanted floors and rats running around at night. Somehow, the magic of the big screen wore off in reality, so I went to my mother, who came up with a welcome idea. By now, I had been able to graduate from UCLA, so she shipped me off to her best friend, Kitty, in the Bay Area. This wonderful woman nourished me with love and inclusiveness in her family of two kids my age while my tummy grew and I waited for the inevitable. I prayed daily on what to do.

So here I was being a passenger in my life again with my parents more or less in charge of my destiny. Perhaps a new beginning would wipe the slate clean as I turned to God for clarity and strength. Having a baby in my stomach was a deeply religious experience. It was somewhat akin to feeling like the Virgin Mary, even though I obviously wasn't a virgin. I walked around with a newly polished halo, or more accurately, a glowing auric field around my whole body, blissfully unaware of the impending personal tragedy ahead.

PING! **Receiving a call from an upscale neighborhood in San Rafael, I was greeted by Betsy, the same lovely elderly woman I remembered picking up a couple of months ago. This doesn't happen very often. But this one was special. When I last saw her, she was suffering from late-stage lymphatic cancer, which she openly talked about then. She had the most positive attitude and was determined to fight it with alternative methods. Now, she told me it had disappeared completely with a special diet eliminating all sugar, processed foods, and other cancer-friendly foods, and by incorporating meditation and yoga into her lifestyle. She had steadfastly refused chemotherapy and radiation and won her battle. Her doctors were amazed.**

She also told me a story of nearly drowning many years ago as a scuba diver. She said they went one night diving off a ship anchored a mile offshore. They each held flashlights while holding the hand of one other person. She let go for a moment to turn on her flashlight, and it slipped out of her hand and fell to the bottom. She lost her scuba mate and was deep under pitch-black water alone. She started praying fervently as she felt her oxygen depleting and frantically waved her arms around. Suddenly she hit the chain of the ship's anchor and was able to pull herself up to the top just in time. She firmly believes she's here for a reason, and I believed I was just graced by an angel. We exchanged cards.

I have always had an interest in metaphysics and spirituality. I was brought up in the Episcopal Church, where I took communion and sang in the choir from the time I was nine. Just before I joined the choir, my next-door neighbor, Susan, a girl my age, was given a whole new wardrobe of beautiful dresses, which she excitedly showed me. I went home green with envy and lay rigid on my bed, praying as hard as I could for God to give me at least three new dresses. I went to my closet and concentrated very hard on visualizing them hanging alongside my other dresses. Then I returned to the bed, praying with my eyes tightly closed and my teeth clenched. I just had to have those dresses! This went on for about two hours from bed to closet and closet to bed, then my mother knocked on the door and said someone wanted to see me.

I opened the door to face Susan, carrying three of her beautiful new dresses on hangers, which she handed to me. Hallelujah! My prayers had been answered! That Sunday I wore one of the dresses to Sunday school and acted as though I was a very special girl graced with a miracle from God, which I would share to everyone's complete and utter amazement. To my complete and utter amazement, no one was impressed—least of all, the Sunday school teacher. In those days, materialism and spiritual manifestations were not talked about in the same breath with religion. It was totally outside of the church's purview and almost blasphemous to put them together in one sentence.

This very special girl was properly put in her place, but at least she had three new dresses and an experience of manifesting through faith and visualization, which was a gift to cherish for the future (a much more open and inclusive future).

Coming back to the precious being growing in my stomach: my father wanted me to keep the baby, so he offered to give me one hundred dollars a month to care for her (an absurd proposition). When I demurred, he had another brilliant idea: to adopt her himself so I could come and visit her as her sister. It was obvious he didn't have any frame of reference for how to manage this situation. So I finally decided to give her up for adoption by the welfare department, and I spent my last month in a home for unwed mothers.

Felicia (the name I gave her meaning "happy") was born September 8, 1964. She had the most beautiful long eyelashes and green eyes. I breastfed her for nine days before letting her go to her new parents. My social worker thought I was mature enough, but it was a huge mistake to allow such bonding to happen. What followed was ten years of depression so deep and painful that I became a social worker myself. It helped me focus solely on others so I could get away from wallowing in my own sorrow. I rattled around in a Honda hatchback acting like Sally Field in *The Flying Nun* from one housing project to another, dispensing the wisdom of a still clueless adult and learning more from my welfare clients than they did from me.

Perhaps, being a spiritual person, I should have experienced that kind of depression after any one of my three abortions, but I didn't. I'm not advocating abortion; this is just my own personal experience. I am suggesting that going full term and giving your child up for adoption is a good option if you think you are strong enough to withstand the emotional pain you may experience. My daughter turned out to be a remarkable woman who has had a wonderful life, being raised by a family who adored and cherished her. She is a wonderful contribution to the world with her amazing singing and acting talent and dedication to combating breast cancer.

In my belief system, there are no accidents, and having an abortion is not an evil act as far as I'm concerned, because it seems perfectly reasonable to believe that the soul does not enter the fetus until well after six months and maybe, in some cases, after he/she is born. Maybe the soul waits until it is sure that it is wanted and is safe. (I know I would.) This belief comes from my absolute conviction that we are reincarnated hundreds and maybe even thousands of times and map out our destinies beforehand on the other side in order to experience situations that will advance our soul's evolution. This would explain why some are born with extreme hardships, such as being born crippled or blind. With this scenario, what would be the point of choosing to be aborted before experiencing your soul's life lesson? Living in California, we are exposed to an array of metaphysical practices, and past-life regressions are a common practice for spiritual seekers.

Past-life regressions are a form of wakeful hypnotism, and one session had me in the eighteenth century as a young male apprentice to the artist Raphael. I saw the streets of Florence vividly. I had never been there, and later that same week, I saw the very same images in a National Geographic magazine. My then mother had me believe that my father was a sea captain who was lost at sea. Somehow word got back to me that my father was actually the local priest. Excited but scared, I paid him a visit to get some sort of confirmation. When I confronted him, he became enraged and bludgeoned me with a fire iron and pushed me into the fire in the fireplace. He called the police and had me hauled off to jail as an intruder. I died in jail from my third-degree burns and remember calling out to my mother, and as I died, I forgave her for deceiving me. It felt like she was someone close to me in this lifetime, perhaps my current mother.

PING! **A short, round-faced, full-figured woman in a long multilayered dress and with a full head of curly white hair, named Misty, stood beside a blue Honda with taillights blinking on the side of the road off the 101. When I pulled up, she smiled brightly and laughingly told me that her beloved Honda pooped out on her. I responded that the taillights still worked pretty well. She giggled and said, "Yes, that's true." She then opened her trunk and pulled out some cloth bags full of embroidered silk fabric and transferred them to my trunk, along with a box of statues, essential oils, a vase and flowers, candleholders, and candles. After turning off the lights and locking her door, she gathered her many layers of clothing around her as she climbed into my back seat. I asked if anyone** was coming to pick up her car, and she replied that she would take care of it later, as it was much more important that she be on time for the workshop she was conducting.

Fascinated, I watched as she pulled a notebook from her shoulder bag and began leafing through it. She stopped and looked up at me and asked if I knew anything about past lives. I responded, "Yes, I've had a few."

She cocked her head, looking askance at me, and giggled again. Her bright blue eyes danced with amusement as she quoted from her notebook: "'Important encounters are planned by the souls long before the bodies see each other.' Do you believe that?" she asked.

I smiled and said, half-chidingly, "So that's why you seemed so familiar to me!"

She squinted her eyes as though a big secret was about to be revealed. "Precisely! Somewhere in time we agreed to meet this way and to touch each other's lives for a brief moment. Isn't it wonderful?" I looked at her through my rearview mirror and saw a woman-child glowing with excitement as she spoke those words.

I asked, "Is this what your workshop is all about?"

She said, "No, but it's a part of what we explore and talk about. We do rituals to clear up any past misgivings and blocks to our happiness, sometimes reaching beyond this present life experience. Life's a mystery, and there is more going on than meets the eye. Only a few will try to see."

She then handed me a brochure with her picture on it and invited me to come to one of her lectures or "healings." "You'll love it, I'm sure!" I told her I would be honored and would look at my schedule to decide the best time to come. She added, "This may be more than just a brief encounter. I can't wait to see what happens next!" She had a satisfied look on her face, as though she knew something I didn't. We arrived at her specified location as she hurriedly gathered her things. I helped carry the box of accouterments inside the hall where about fifty or sixty people were mingling. They looked up when we came through the door, and several ran to her side to hug her and help carry her bags. She introduced me as her "very special Uber driver," and they all nodded knowingly. As I left, I couldn't help but feel I had been uplifted to another level of awareness and self-love.

10

SOMEWHERE OVER THE RAINBOW

A Lesson in Miracles

In 1969, five years after Felicia's birth, a friend told me that if I chanted "Nam Myo Ho Renge Kyo" and took two aspirins, I could cure any headache. Not seeing the irony in this, I became interested and attended a meeting. Right away, I signed up and became a Nichiren Shoshu Buddhist. This particular sect advocated celibacy and free everything (but love) just for chanting the mantra and doing the Lotus Sutra recitation twice a day.

For thirteen years I atoned for all my sins, chanting two to three hours a day, leading meetings, enlisting other "unhappy" souls, and helping them get their lives back as well. I abstained from dating for almost eleven of those thirteen years. Total celibacy and devotion from 6 a.m. to 12 a.m. every day was rewarded by "You can have anything you want if you just chant 'Nam Myo Ho Renge Kyo.'" They forgot to tell me that *love* was not in the equation. I should have seen the red flag when I excitedly showed a senior leader an unexpected love letter from my fifteen-year obsession (Basil) requesting I spend a week with him in Puerto Vallarta because "we deserve some time together." But she, in no uncertain terms, told me to reject the offer and focus only on my practice.

Thus the final curtain came down on Basil St. John, the man of my dreams. He did show up briefly thirty years later, completely destroyed by booze, the fire gone from his bloodshot eyes and his stomach distended from an inflamed liver. Although he was happy to see me, he was perpetually angry with everyone and everything, barking orders at bartenders and waitresses. He confessed that he was scared because he was constantly fighting vertigo, thinking he would black out at any moment He said he never remarried. (OMG, was I to blame for this?) He died a few years later. I cried when I reread his sweet letter, which had been forgotten and in storage for thirty-five years. It was the only significant love letter I ever received from anyone.

One of the major tenets of this branch of Buddhism was regarding "karma," or cause and effect. According to its tenets, most everything in one's life that occurs repeatedly and cannot be explained through psychology or any other means is caused by karma. I was instilled with the belief that chanting would help to change my karma from a cheap B-movie to a blockbuster hit. I thought surely I could change my karma with men, which is why I stuck with it for thirteen years and vigorously chanted for hours every day, losing my singing voice in the process.

Later in my life I had a clear vision of who I was in a recent past life, which could explain my karma with men. I saw myself as an unknown artist in Paris paling around with Degas, Cezanne, and Toulouse-Lautrec while I used beautiful women for my paintings. I would callously use and seduce them, dismissing them as soon as I got what I wanted, causing many broken hearts.

Although I was never able to see any noticeable results from chanting that changed my love karma, throughout my thirteen years of Buddhist practice, I had several unexplained miracles and a myriad of "benefits" that kept hope alive.

While the religion itself explains the miracles as proof of the power of chanting, remembering my childhood experience of manifesting, I have come to the conclusion that all thoughts are powerful, and if you spend enough time and energy with one thought, you can easily put into action its manifestation. It's called the "Law of Attraction," or the power of intention. Why didn't it work for my man karma? I now believe that my intention for love has always been blocked by my fear of commitment and ultimately rejection and abandonment after giving myself away completely to my first love. This fear was born from observing my mother and father's relationship and later cemented in my subconscious mind by Basil and Nameless and countless others. Chanting never brought this awareness to light. I always assumed it was just really bad karma. However, the belief that this chant is a positive and powerful vibration is cause enough for great things to happen that aren't necessarily on your wish list. It keeps you ever hopeful that eventually your wishes will be fulfilled.

For instance, driving home from a meeting in Hollywood late one night, I didn't notice that I was being followed. When I stopped and parked my car, my car door on the driver's side suddenly flew open, and a young black man held a knife to my neck and demanded I give him all my money. Strangely, I felt no fear. I looked him squarely in the eyes in a moment of realized compassion and said, "You don't have to do this. All you need to do is chant NAM MYO HO RENGE KYO [I said it with the full force of a lion's roar, which is how I normally chant] and you can have anything you want." The poor guy thought I was doing some kind of voodoo on him, backed away with his eyes bulging out of his head, ran in a full sprint back to his car, and laid some rubber as he sped away.

Once, I had a flat tire on Hollywood Boulevard in front of a tire store. I bought a new tire and enlisted a young man walking by on the sidewalk to install it for me. Turns out I got the wrong rim attached to the tire, which had four lug nut holes while my wheel had five. I didn't understand or care, so I chanted as hard and sincerely as I could even though this young cynic laughed and said it was virtually impossible. And then *bam*! It went on. He couldn't believe it and, with that, was enrolled and came with us to the meeting.

Once while speeding down the Harbor Freeway at eighty miles per hour, trying to make a meeting on time, I was stopped by a cop. I frantically told him where I was going and why it was so important. Silly me. Could I be so naive to think he cared? Turns out he did. He sighed and said, "Oh, I understand. My wife belongs to the same Buddhism," and he let me go without a ticket.

PING! Standing on the corner of Van Ness and Lombard was an older couple that looked uncannily like someone I used to know. Indeed, turns out it was my Buddhist district chief from forty years ago, Stan, and his wife, Norma, who had gotten married in the wedding dress I designed and made for her in 1972. During their secret courtship, I remember how smitten he was with her, calling on her to speak first whenever she raised her hand at meetings. Their obvious attraction to each other was adorable to watch since it really was one of the few love stories going on in the Buddhist organization at the time. They now have two married daughters and several grandchildren. They had just flown in from Carson City, Nevada, and were taking in the San Francisco sights for the weekend. Looking at them through my rearview mirror, I marveled at how they still seemed smitten with each other, holding hands while he laughed delightedly at her insightfully funny comments.

Looking out the window at all the pedestrians, Stan asked, "Why is everyone so young and skinny here? Is it their diet?"

She said, "Oh yes, I heard this is really a retirement town for old geezers like us, but they all eat greens five times a day so they look twenty or thirty years younger. That's why we're here—so we can get some of them greens!"

With that he drew her close to him and kissed her sweetly and said, "Honey, you don't need them greens. You still look good to me!"

"Oh, Stan." She laughed demurely as she returned the kiss. "You're such a tease!" And I got all goosepimply!

Chanting causes you to think you are doing something powerful and positive for your life, so it becomes a very pleasurable and secure feeling while you chant. You innately believe that you are invoking the power of the gods to do your bidding. These days the urge to chant when an unpleasant situation occurs has been replaced with the mantra of intention, like the one I invoked at the beginning of this book. I find that my sincerity in connecting to Source or acknowledging my own higher self is all I need to create miracles in my life.

I have many dear friends still practicing this Buddhism and I honor their compassion and sincerely held belief and the work they continue to do for the betterment of the world. Tina Turner, Patrick Duffy, and Herbie Hancock practice it, and at one time, the entire Dodger baseball team did as well.

This practice had a built-in motivator that continually enticed me to stick with it, by the small miracles I attributed to it every day. Some were bigger than others, such as the plane fare for four pilgrimages to Japan showing up in my mailbox. Money always seemed to show up for whatever I needed at the time.

Every two or three years, we looked forward to a group *Tozan* (pilgrimage) to Japan. The headquarters in Tokyo, headed by President Daisaku Ikeda, was responsible for building a huge modern glass-and-concrete earthquake-proof temple called Daisekiji at the foot of Mt. Fuji, surrounded by lush grounds and group-housing buildings. This temple housed the Dai Gohonzon scroll, which was the original object of worship scribed by Nichiren Daishonin in thirteenth-century Japan. We each were given our own smaller personal Gohonzons at our induction ceremonies. We ascribed great power to our Gohonzons and especially to the Dai Gohonzon as being a direct line to God, or God "Itself." I remember sitting in the great hall facing the altar where the Dai Gohonzon was enshrined, expecting to be thrown into another dimension as soon as they opened the doors of the shrine to reveal the great scroll. Well, nothing happened, but I pretended it did like everyone else.

I attended four Tozans, one for each season. My first Tozan was in summer, and we were hit with hot, humid weather, which could be managed only by carrying a cool wet facecloth and a Japanese fan. I purchased my first kimono, a blue-and-white cotton print, and proudly wore it downtown, only to be met with averted eyes and embarrassed snickers. I found out later that what I was wearing was a traditional bathrobe. The other clothes item I purchased was pantyhose, which I again found out later were impossible to wear because the crotch came up only as far as my knees. We Americans were like uncultured giants in this beautiful, serene foreign land of "little" people.

My longest Tozan was a month in winter where we split up into groups of three—a man, a woman, and a translator— and were driven to different members' homes throughout Japan. We were given the assignment to speak about our American experience to large groups assembled in different meeting places every night. I found this to be a wonderful experience, as the Japanese were extremely gracious and appreciative of us.

Winter was especially challenging, as most homes did not have central heating, and the preferred method of warming up was jumping into a scalding hot tub after hand bathing on a stool in front of a faucet in the basement. The water in the tub was so hot you jumped in and out faster than a Looney Tunes Roadrunner, and your temperature was sufficiently raised to keep you warm through the night. Being minimalists, most Japanese homes stored their dining tables, floor pillows (chairs), mattresses, and bedding in closets and brought them out when needed. The tables had heaters under them to keep your lower body warm, and butane heaters were placed around us to keep our upper bodies warm. My most ingratiating and at the same time perplexing experience was the time I was invited to someone's home for tea and I happened to comment on one of their ceramic bowls as being particularly beautiful. As is customary, they insisted I take it. I was thrown for a loop and didn't know how to react. Unfortunately, I ended up rejecting their generosity out of pure ignorance.

Back home, this Buddhism was a very difficult and demanding practice. I developed muscles I never had before, including self-discipline, unrelenting faith, letting go of ego, surrendering to a higher power or wisdom, and becoming fearless in learning how to approach strangers and enroll them into this discipline. All these muscles have played a big role in everything I've accomplished in life thus far.

I think maybe the most relevant benefit I got from this practice was my evolving into a compassionate and caring human being. I worked tirelessly with my district of fifty or so members, encouraging them to keep practicing in the face of seemingly insurmountable obstacles. Every day on the street and through my social work, I enlisted people into the practice. Being a social worker in LA County was a perfect training ground for leadership in the Buddhist organization.

One time on my rounds, I attempted to enlist one of my family welfare clients in the housing projects. Josie was like the walking (or in this case, sitting) dead. Her kids ran around half-naked, snot dripping from their noses, in an apartment with orange crates for furniture except for the large TV and easy chair in the living room. At first she was completely unresponsive (picture a fat woman slouched in her chair with eyes half-closed and mouth hanging open), but finally, I got her to chant. Let's just say that six months later, she had gone to school to learn a vocation, then got a job, got off welfare, got thinner, and became one of my most enthusiastic and vivacious members and eventually a leader herself. Go see a movie starring Leslie Jones and you will get an accurate picture of Josie's transformation.

Another memorable incident was when I went to the hospital to see one of my welfare clients who had tried to commit suicide. She was strapped down on a gurney. I took her hand, looked into her eyes, and told her that right now she was lucky because she could still make choices. If she were dead, she couldn't. And you never know what opportunities will come your way the next day. I went on to tell her about some opportunities that came my way just when I thought there was no hope. And, of course, I told her about Nam Myo Ho Renge Kyo.

One year later she visited me at the office to say that that was a life-changing encounter for her, as she was then able to pick herself up, get off of drugs, and become a completely new person because of it.

PING! **It was late and I wanted to go home when I answered a call, hoping it would be a short, local ride. Approaching the car was a young man in a wool beanie with a million tattoos on his upper body half-covered by a cropped-off T-shirt. He emerged from an upscale house in Marin and wanted to go to San Francisco to pick up something and then use me to ride back home.** *Oh-oh . . . not a good sign.* **Was I going to take part in an errant son's dope score? I heard him talk on the phone, asking if two hundred dollars was enough, and if not, he could possibly do three hundred dollars. I pretended not to be listening and asked him where we were going and why we were going there. He looked at me and smiled a crooked smile, which I found out later was due to an ear operation that went bad, causing half his face to be paralyzed. He said it was a surprise for his little brother, who had meningitis and had just come home from the hospital. I thought,** *Oh, here it goes. He's going to tell me he's picking up some special medicine for his brother, and I'm to believe it.*

An hour later we arrived at a house on the outskirts of San Francisco near Daly City. He asked me to wait and he'd be right back. A moment later he came out carrying a duffle bag with a fabric screen on one end. Turns out it was a puppy carrier housing a small pug with a scrunched-up face, the cutest little dog I've ever seen. I was very impressed and at the same time ashamed of my completely wrong assumptions. He said the dog's name was Rocky, because his brother loved all the Rocky movies on Netflix. *Damn! I was way off!*

"Never judge a book by its cover" is so appropriate. I have often been delightfully surprised by the people I pick up on my Uber rounds after engaging in meaningful conversations that reveal their true essence to me. I think everyone has a transformed Josie hiding out somewhere inside. It just takes a little prodding to pull her out.

Back in the late sixties and seventies, our Buddhist headquarters in LA had a very charismatic leader from Korea named Masayasu Sadanaga, later self-named George M. Williams, who was uncommonly handsome. We were drawn to his youthful energy and his strong belief that this Buddhism held the key to world peace. He had a vivid imagination and created events to spread the word in a spectacular manner. When I think back, I'm amazed at what we created under his direction.

We had huge conventions every summer, but one year in particular stood out. It was in 1968 in Honolulu, Hawaii, and it took a whole year in Santa Monica and Hawaii to prepare for this. We created a parade with floats, our brass band, our bagpipe band, our fife-and-drum corps, and hundreds of dancers who marched down the main street of Honolulu the day before our convention. That same day we put on a performance in front of thirty thousand sunbathers, after having built a fake island with a stage and a smoking volcano facing the main beach in Honolulu. Removable sets were made representing major cultures and countries around the world, and dancers performed in costumes representing India, Russia, Ireland, Africa, Switzerland, England, France, and many others. Costumed swimmers performed in an aquacade around the floating stage. It was a gargantuan effort.

I spent my entire three days in Hawaii in a fume-filled warehouse putting the final touches on the floats. Upon arriving in Hawaii, we had been herded (like cattle to the slaughter) into our "waterfront hotel," which was, in essence, a converted shipyard dock with one thousand cots side by side and dozens of mobile toilets at one end.

Why we didn't spend the money and arrange to stay in the many hotels available there, I don't know. I would have been more than happy to pay for it after one night in that hellhole shit house (literally). But we chanted together and overcame (so we convinced ourselves). We were very good at convincing ourselves that we were the chosen ones out to save the world, and any discomfort was well worth the sacrifice. Holding such huge momentous events was a way to enroll converts on a grand scale, not to mention reenrolling ourselves.

Our enthusiasm built upon itself. Our group dynamic portrayed the spirit of extreme happiness and good fortune to each other and to all whom we invited into the fold. We inspired everyone with our wondrous testimonials. We patted each other and ourselves on the back every chance we got. There was a very good reason for this. As I stated earlier, this was a very difficult practice. It brought us face to face with our demons, our weaknesses, and our guilty pasts while highlighting our dreams and hopes for the future. It created expectations that sometimes did not meet reality. At those times, we sought guidance and encouraging words from our senior leaders.

Part of the appeal of this practice was the possibility of being appointed to a high leadership position through a strong practice. For thirteen years, my dream of becoming a senior leader was forever stymied. I was only one step below as a district chief (*Chikutan*) but miles away in reality from the privileges and accessibility to certain events and higher leaders, like Mr. Williams and President Ikeda. I became a Chikutan within the first three months of my practice. After that, for some unknown reason I was never appointed to a higher position, even though my practice was strong and unwavering and my members were thriving under my leadership. I was given a clue when my *Sochibucho* (general chapter chief) demeaned me in front of my district, calling me "obsequious, unlike [one of my Honcho assistants] Marilyn, who is a true leader." One year after I left, he was called out and reprimanded for his mean-spirited arrogance toward hundreds of his members. *Obsequious*: the epitome of victimhood. I hated that word because it was true.

Looking back, their guidance system was, at times, dysfunctional. Sometimes power was given to those who had their own personal agendas and little or no wisdom or real compassion for their members. They covered themselves by saying that we should surrender to their guidance even if it didn't feel right, because we would get the benefit anyway by following in faith. In many instances, this was true, but in other cases, this should be a warning to anyone joining a religious organization that promises to change your life miraculously if you blindly follow the advice of their leader(s). There is a fine line between surrendering in faith and giving away your power. So always check in and make that distinction, even if it means going against the dictates of the organization and being rejected. Think of Jonestown.

The saving grace of this Buddhist practice is the practice of chanting itself, which is a form of meditation that will, more often than not, allow you to access your own higher knowing and will lead you to your desired state of being.

However, this sect of Buddhism couldn't give me any satisfactory answers for my lack of a loving partnership, which is ironic since I began chanting mostly for the purpose of finding true love. Compassion was the operative word, not love. In all the teachings, love was barely mentioned, and when it was, it was deemed unworthy of discussion. According to this sect, love is an illusion. That certainly was right; in my case, it was nothing but an illusion.

Year after year, my demeanor was less and less enthusiastic as I was constantly held back from achieving my dream of leadership or having an intimate loving relationship. By the time I reached year thirteen, I was suicidal, so I sought the help of a psychologist rather than another ineffective or mean-spirited senior leader.

PING! My first pickup of the day was a Latino guy named Renaldo, wanting to go to Richmond for a get-together with his

family and friends. He talked about how hard it was to work twelve to fourteen hours a day just to make ends meet but had faith that somehow everything would work out for him and his family. He then brought up an amazing story about being despondent and committing suicide when he was a teenager. That's right, he did not *attempt* to commit suicide; he actually committed suicide.

He described it like this:"I made a hangman's noose and put it over my head and under my chin. I kicked the chair from under me and suddenly couldn't breathe, and I panicked, trying to get out of the noose. I then felt all my energy leave my body as I began to lose consciousness. At that point I said, "Forgive me, God," and just before I blacked out, the rope was cut and I fell to the floor. There was no one there. It was a perfectly good rope, but it was cut in half. You're the only person I have told this to. I haven't told my wife or kids. They wouldn't understand, but somehow I knew you would. I truly believe in God and try every day to encourage others to believe. He saved my life." I then told him about my out-of-body experience, which was a gift to let me know I was not my body. At the end of the ride, he took my hand in both of his and said thank you and then reached over to hug me. I cried and couldn't pick up any more riders. He touched me so deeply.

11

HAPPY DAYS ARE HERE AGAIN
In La-La Land

A few years before I imploded and sought guidance from a psychologist, I had my most amazing Buddhist miracle yet: I was hired as head of wardrobe at CBS from out of the blue. After four years of being a social worker, I was hired at Angelica Uniform Company, where I worked for five years as their designer for California uniform clients. During my fifth year there, I worked alongside a known TV designer who was using our company for a Hilton Hotel uniform project. My job was to help him find the right fabric and findings for his designs. One day he told me that the head of wardrobe at CBS had resigned and that there was an opening, which he thought I should pursue. Other than him, I didn't know anyone currently in the business, and I had never worked with costumes or wardrobe in TV. I was just a uniform designer who chanted, and when they interviewed me for the job, somehow they liked me. They also liked my sketches of designs for Cher, which I made especially for the interview.

I landed the job after a week of interviews. To give you an idea of how it goes in showbiz, my last interview was two hours long. I sat through a long, rapturous narrative about my interviewee's handsome grown son, never being asked one question about myself. I suppose because I was such a polite and seemingly interested listener, she (Rosemary) thought I was the perfect candidate for the job.

My first week at CBS began with an hour-long bonus show by Sammy Davis Jr. for all CBS staff and employees. I remember wishing I had the courage to go up to him and personally thank him. The next day while I was on the set of *The Young and the Restless* watching rehearsals, I suddenly turned to see Sammy Davis Jr. standing right behind me, and at that moment I was able to thank him for his generosity.

There were many moments like that in the halls and studios of CBS, like passing George Burns (otherwise known as "God") in the hall as he tipped his hat to me, or watching the unruly teenage gang from the Jackson Five family taking orders from their youngest, Michael, who was grounded and mature by comparison. My biggest thrill was meeting Bob Mackey, the designer for all of Cher's incredible costumes. He was my original inspiration to apply for the job when I submitted my own designs as a way to get noticed.

Being the head of wardrobe put me in the position to take charge of the whole wardrobe for *The Young and the Restless,* and for any other shows that needed readymade clothes from local shops or costumes designed and made in our department.

My first work challenge came when the CEO of Giorgio's Beverly Hills, hearing that a "neophyte" had replaced the head of wardrobe at CBS, decided to charge us for the gorgeous clothes CBS had been able to rent free of charge for years, just for the publicity. I knew nothing about Giorgio's nor had any experience in negotiating contracts. So, thinking I was doing CBS a huge favor, I canceled the contract with Giorgio's and sought to find another free source of clothes for our *Y&R* cast. This was the beginning of the end of my CBS job, as I substituted Giorgio's with Buffum's Department Store, a ridiculously inadequate replacement. Giorgio was in a class all by itself, with designer dresses costing thousands of dollars in Beverly Hills. Buffum's then was like Macy's is now. Somehow I managed to find a few good items every week to mollify the producer and put off the inevitable.

Another challenge came when I had the opportunity to design the wardrobe for a comedy pilot called *Husbands and Wives* involving the foibles of six suburban couples, produced by Joan Rivers and her husband Edgar Rosenberg. This was my true initiation into the world of TV costuming. Besides catering to the wishes of twelve prima-donna stars, I had to balance the wishes of two different executive producers who had two different ideas, and also a director, an assistant director, and a stage manager, all with different ideas and demands. Each one would tell me in strict confidence to ignore the others' suggestions or demands. My head was spinning, and I was out of breath running from store to store and trying several different versions for each star for each scene. In the end everything worked out OK, even though the last garment I found to replace another came in the middle of the taping just before that person came on with her scene. Such is the world of showbiz. It is a world where egos collide, but in the end, with a "lil' bit o' luck," perfection is obtained.

Here are a few quotes from Joan that I have to include to honor her memorable comedic brilliance:

I don't exercise. If God had wanted me to bend over, he would have put diamonds on the floor.

People say that money is not the key to happiness, but I always figured if you have enough money, you can have a key made.

I wish I had a twin, so I could know what I'd look like without plastic surgery.

While we're at it, guess who was starring in a comedy series at CBS: Nameless the Clown himself! But my low self-esteem had built a huge protective wall around my heart, so I could regard him only with cold ambivalence mixed with unwarranted awe for his celebrity status. I was awkward and he was arrogant, especially for a nameless clown.

There were many times I felt out of place at CBS, thinking I had cheated by chanting to get the job instead of being adequately qualified. My lack of confidence in myself was reflected in my reaction to Nameless. When I came face to face with him, there was none of the intimate connection we once had. Now he was a complete stranger to me.

I should mention that during this time my father had remarried again, but this time to my cousin (yes, cousin on his side), who was thirteen years younger than me and forty years younger than Dad (he sixty-four, she twenty-four). His last wife had become an alcoholic, much like my mother, who had developed migraines and epilepsy. How ironic that he was a doctor who made the women close to him sick. This last one was a little bit smarter. She was intact when she left him in the middle of the night after seventeen years of abuse. But it destroyed him. He got very old very fast and died two years later.

Life in the fast lane at CBS got to be a bit too much for this three-wheeled buggy, with the in-house politics and my own inexperience getting me fired after only a year. But I had a good enough driving record to succeed as an independent costumer at other major studios for five more years. It was an exciting time, and my self-esteem got back on track.

PING! **Pulling up to the Marriott Hotel in San Francisco, I see a crowd of mostly tall, beautiful women dressed in cocktail dresses and evening gowns. One of them spots me and waves her arm enthusiastically to get my attention. She pulls two other friends with her and climbs in the front seat while they occupy the back seat. My car is suddenly enveloped in a mixture of three strong perfumes as the lady in the front seat peers at me from under long false eyelashes and says in a deep masculine voice, "Hi, honey, how are you? I'm Marci, the one who called you."**

I noticed immediately that I felt self-conscious and awkward in this new reality. They were on a happy high and soon ingratiated themselves, making me feel I was accepted as one of them. Their *joi de vivre* attitude was striking, as was their dramatic makeup and glamorous clothing. They explained that they were at a transgender convention and had made friends with each other only that day. I couldn't help cracking up at their hilarious observations of straight people who were skittish around them. With every comment they would start with the word *honey* and try to outdo each other with outrageous descriptions, like, "Honey, did you catch the short, fat guy adjusting his toupee when he grinned and said "hi" to us in the elevator?" to which another chimed in, "Oh, honey, he was so cute. I wanted to pull it off and kiss his adorable bald head." They howled with laughter, and then they asked if I would like to join them for a drink. I was truly touched and honored by their generous invitation and thanked them but said no, I needed to work. I often wonder what it would have been like if I had said yes. It was probably a missed opportunity.

Every show I worked on was a family affair. We all became bonded like a close-knit family, from the biggest star and supporting actors to the stagehands and costumers. One thing we all had in common was being happy to be working. A deep sense of gratitude was our glue. The other was the gift of creativity we all shared and respected in one another. We knew we were each a relevant part of a team that was creating a singular work of art.

Two of my favorite shows were *Happy Days* with Henry Winkler and Ron Howard and *Laverne and Shirley* with Penny Marshall and Cindy Williams, both done at Paramount Studios. At that time, Robin Williams was an up-and-coming star working on *Mork and Mindy*. A couple of times he came to watch our *Laverne and Shirley* tapings when he was done taping his show on another soundstage. Once, he and Penny, Cindy, and I inhaled helium balloons and cracked each other up talking in high-pitched cartoon voices. We were all blown away by his quick off-the-wall wit with or without the helium.

One of my favorite Buddhists, Patrick Duffy, who was just an up-and-coming actor when I knew him, asked me to babysit for him and his wife in his dingy old roach-infested apartment above Hollywood Boulevard. He gave me a script to read that he had just gotten the lead part in, *The Man from Atlantis*, and asked me what I thought of it. Two years later, after only one season of *The Man from Atlantis*, he got a starring role as Bobby in *Dallas*, and I had the good fortune to be assigned to the show as the female costume coordinator at MGM for a few months. (A side note: Patrick and I took on Hollywood Boulevard one night to do *Shakabuku*, which is the Japanese word for enrolling strangers into coming to a Buddhist meeting. He was really good at it. I marveled at his ability to connect to perfect strangers.)

Patrick also had a lightning-quick sense of humor, which he demonstrated with Larry Hagman in the outtakes. In between sets, while some of the crew were setting up for the next scene, they would reenact the last scene as a satire, hilariously and brilliantly ad-libbing to the delight of an audience of attentive cast and crewmembers.

In four years, I had done dozens of movies and TV shows. By this time I was a Costumer 2, and my big break came as the head designer/costumer of a TV series that I was particularly fond of called *Another Day* with David Groh and Joan Hackett. This was done in front of a live audience at Warner Bros. but lasted only one season.

I created a style of clothing for Joan that was classy and unique. She often wore hats that outlined her adorably expressive face and sometimes had a feather that drooped down and tickled her nose, causing spontaneous laughter from the audience. Joan had a whimsical charm all her own, but she was in constant competition with David, who, she insisted, tried to upstage her at every opportunity. She displayed a deep inferiority complex that had her acting out as the quintessential prima donna, fighting the director and the writers during every rehearsal. She sometimes flew into a rage and walked out. I had to constantly soothe her ruffled feathers with exaggerated compliments to get her back on track. She was the undisputed star of the show with her exceptional acting ability and comedic sense. Sadly, she died a few years later of ovarian cancer.

Right after *Another Day*, I was asked to be the head designer of *Flo*, a spinoff of *Alice*, with Polly Holliday at Warner Bros. This was also done before a live audience.

Designing for *Flo* was categorically the opposite of my work for *Another Day*. Flo's wardrobe consisted of flashy spandex pants and sheer ruffled blouses in bright colors. She pranced around like a peacock, saying things like "Kiss ma grits!" in her southern twang.

PING! Four rowdy twenty-something women dressed in white cocktail dresses in midafternoon squeezed their oversized bodies into my car. I asked why they were all wearing white, to which they replied with an air of importance that it was an all-white dress party (*Stupid me*, I thought sarcastically!). To add to the ambiance, one of them turned on a loud rock music station on her iPhone, and they all talked simultaneously to each other in louder screeching tones. Regrettably, my app indicated that I had forty-eight minutes to go with them as they were headed toward Pier 1 at the Embarcadero in San Francisco. They squealed with excitement about the boat ride they were going to take. At one point I covered my ears and asked if they could take it down a notch, which they did for about thirty seconds.

Tamara, the heftiest and loudest girl of the bunch, sat in the front seat in her very tight and very short mini-dress and immediately put the visor mirror down so she could adjust her headband, her long corkscrew curls, her eyelashes, and other parts of her face in between taking selfies with the girls in the back seat. At last count, she did this eight times throughout the whole ride. I,

unfortunately, could find no redeeming qualities in any of the girls as they blathered on about how many hours it took to dress that day, talking over each other to add to the volume. It seemed they were competing for who took the longest. They squealed, screeched, and howled with the loud rock music for all of forty-eight minutes, and I thought to myself, *Why me, God? Wasn't my prayer of intention sincere enough for you today?* Happily, I arrived right on time, and one of the girls said, "You're a really good driver. Thank you for getting us here safely and on time," to which the others agreed vociferously. *Hmmmm . . . OK, God, I get it. Maybe if I had been a little less judgmental, I might have enjoyed the ride.*

I find that I still struggle with my over-activated judgmental nature. Being an artist and a photographer with somewhat high standards of beauty, when I see extremely overweight women dressing and acting as if they're size-two supermodels in search of a talent agent, I get a little crazy. This tells me I'm still a stretch away from my goal of self-love.

Throughout this period, besides loving the work I was doing and still practicing Buddhism, I began delving into metaphysics and attending channelings. One day while taking an afternoon nap, something extraordinary happened. It was my first out-of-body experience: I was in the middle of a dream in which I drove to our set at Warner Bros. and got a handful of clothes on hangers out of my trunk and followed Polly Holliday into the soundstage. I followed her through the audience risers to the stage and then backstage, where I saw her disappear through a door. I went to the door and opened it to find another door immediately behind it, then four more doors, until I got to the last one, which was just a half a door. I burst out laughing and said, "Do you call yourself a door?" With that I was immediately transported into a scene that was more real than reality itself. I found myself lifting off the ground and then flying as the landscape whizzed by until I was high in the blue sky looking down at a valley nestled between beautiful green hills with cows and winding roads and small cottages (pretty much like where I live today). Then suddenly blackness was closing in, and the scene was getting smaller and farther away. . . . I cried out, "Please let me stay here a little longer!" and a male voice said, "No, it's time for you to go back now." With that I was suddenly plunked down into my body, but the scariest part was, I didn't know how to open my eyes for several seconds.

I have always thought this to be a gift to let me know I am not my body and that life will go on and may be even more beautiful and strikingly real after death. I have heard and read so many personal accounts of life after death, and my friend Dannion Brinkley personally recounted his first near-death experience to me. Dannion is an author who is well known for his three near-death experiences, two of which were caused by lightning, with the first one rendering him clinically dead for twenty-eight minutes. He returned to his body, which was already in a body bag, after quite an "enlightening" experience in the afterlife. His experiences and spiritual awakening are well documented in his books: *Saved by the Light*, *At Peace in the Light*, and *Secrets of the Light*. He has had numerous guest appearances on TV talk shows.

Meanwhile, I was still practicing Buddhism and effectively still celibate, even with all the temptations at hand in this made-for-TV world. So, not only sex but also love was still elusive. Chanting for thirteen years had gotten me nowhere on that score, and I was still unconsciously attracted to married men and they to me. I remember the first time I kissed someone at a cast party while I was still celibate. I connected with the assistant director, and after our first kiss, we decided to go to his car and make out in the back seat. He and I continued kissing in the back seat of his car for hours until the break of dawn. I couldn't stop and neither could he. We sucked each other's faces off, but we never went any further. I think I was finally satiated after eleven years of being a nun. My life was not a blockbuster hit yet, but at least my B-movie was a little more interesting and had the potential of being nominated for a technical Oscar: the longest pre-sex kiss in cinematic history. Did anything ever come of this? No. In the light of day, the magic wore off, and we both went our separate ways.

12

I'M A BELIEVER

My Fate Was Sealed When I Saw His Face

By the time I was forty, I was desperate for a single man to love and went to see a psychologist, who gave me three books to read. *Be Here Now* and *Grist for the Mill* by Ram Dass and *Hammer on the Rock* by Bhagwan Shree Rajneesh (later known as Osho). I think he sensed it was time for me to look outside of Buddhism for the answer. Yep, uh-huh, I was ready!

Bhagwan's book *Hammer on the Rock* was actually a chisel that broke through the brick wall around my heart and let some light in. Upon reading the first paragraph of the first chapter of that book, I fell madly in love again, but this time from afar, with a spiritual master. What delivered the final love blow was a tape I heard later on the word *fuck*, which he lectured on for twenty minutes in his inimitably refined manner of speech. It began, "*Fuck*, is the most beautiful word in the English language. Let me tell you why," and he listed all the ways it could be used grammatically. My sides hurt from laughing so hard, and after eleven years of celibacy, I knew I had to go to India to sit at his feet and begin the next stage of my development.

Being impatient for self-gratification, I wasted no time dying all my clothes red, and those I couldn't dye, I gave away. This was the color assigned to his neo-sannyasins (disciples), worn along with the mala (a beaded necklace with his portrait in a wooden locket) as a symbol of surrendering the ego to the higher self via our guide and catalyst, Bhagwan. Impatient for instant gratification, I went to a bead store and bought 108 dark wooden beads and a cheap gold-tone locket. I then found a magazine with Bhagwan's picture, and when I cut it out, it fit perfectly into the locket. Having strung the beads together with the locket, I solemnly put the "mala" around my neck and proudly became a self-made Rajneesh sannyasin.

My first encounter with the Rajneesh community was with a gorgeous, tan, long-blond-haired sannyasin named Swami James at the Bodhi Tree Bookstore in Beverly Hills. He came home with me, and we made love with our eyes. We sat cross-legged on the floor facing each other and looking deep into each other's eyes. We focused on matching the rhythm of our breaths. This was my first taste of tantric foreplay.

Then after reading a few of Bhagwan's books, I took a trip to a place called Geetam in the high desert in San Bernardino near Victorville. This was a small, bustling Rajneesh community living high on life and love in a privately guarded desert paradise unbeknownst to anyone but those who sought to know. Driving up the driveway, I was not prepared for what I saw: handsome, long-haired, half-naked men and women walking around unselfconsciously doing odd jobs. One older man wearing only a tool belt/apron got my attention when I noticed his "member" hanging below the apron. Well, granted, it was a hot day in the desert, but coming from eleven years of celibacy and a rigid social structure, this was a complete shock to my nervous system. However, something about everyone's authenticity melted my resistance, and I quickly assimilated into this new culture, especially when that old man turned around to reveal an adorable bare bottom.

PING! I picked up a tall, lanky guy with gray hair and kind eyes in Novato who wanted to go to Good Earth in Fairfax. He looked

very familiar, and then I knew he was a sannyasin I'd often seen at *satsang* (Sunday morning home meditations and potluck). We exchanged hellos, reintroducing ourselves, and I asked him if he knew about the book called *93 Rolls-Royces*, written by Deva Peter Haykus, which was about the last days of Bhagwan at the ranch in Oregon called Rajneeshpuram. He looked bewildered and said, "No. What is it about?" I giggled at his obvious faux pas and said, "Well, I think it's about ninety-three Rolls-Royces." Sheepishly he nodded and smiled. There was very little ego evident in this man, who was like a gentle giant. He asked what I was up to, and I told him I was writing a book about Uber driving and that I might put him in my book. He laughed and then said, "That'd be different," which was true to his unassuming nature.

After sending Bhagwan a letter about why I wanted to take *sannyas*, (become a disciple), I received a letter back from him giving me my new name, Ma Veet Yamini, with an explanation of its meaning—"going beyond the night into a life of consciousness," which was my dharma (spiritual path). I was then given the official sannyas ceremony at Geetam, officiated by Krishna Prem, a sannyasin I had gotten to know and love. And so a real mala took the place of my silly homemade one. It was accepted that all shades of red or orange were the only colors we could wear as Rajneesh sannyasins. I was already ahead of the game with all my newly dyed clothes.

By this time, I was right in the middle of one of my proudest achievements as the wardrobe designer of the *Flo* TV series at Warner Bros. This was a spinoff of the *Alice* show with Linda Lavin, where Polly Holliday first played the character Flo. Right after my trip to Geetam, I made arrangements to go to India, even though the show was not finished with its first season.

I rolled up my *Gohonzon* (sacred object of worship scroll), gave it back to my senior leaders, packed my bags, and left for India with my shades-of-red wardrobe and my new name and mala. Before I left, the credits on *Flo* now showed my name as Ma Veet Yamini. When I told my boss Rita Riggs that I was leaving for India before the end of the season, she sarcastically said, "Whatever gets you through the night." How synchronistic . . . she had no idea how close she came to accurately describing the meaning of my name.

I was sorry to leave my family on the *Flo* show, as I was to leave my Buddhist family. Time to join a new tribe that resonated with my soul's purpose.

Being the romantic dreamer that I was, I packed everything into a large trunk that I thought would be needed for an infinite number of years in India. There were no thoughts of ever returning to America. I was a "lifer" for Bhagwan. But nothing had prepared me for what I was to encounter when I got to India. The plane landed around 2 a.m., and I shared a taxi with two other sannyasins to go from Bombay (now Mumbai) to Pune, which was about a five-hour drive. Little boy beggars followed me to the car and tapped on the window while a policeman batted them way with his billy club. I looked apologetically at them through the window, confused and shocked by the brutality.

Pulling out of the airport, our cab picked up speed to about eighty miles per hour without any headlights on and drove down a long narrow unlit country road that stretched for hundreds of miles. This was very unnerving, but what we saw along the way made it pale by comparison. We saw overturned trucks with bodies of people strewn about. I would guesstimate that we saw at least three such incidents that night. My cabbie didn't pay any attention and quickly sped by. Then we were stopped by uniformed police at two different posts who asked to inspect our baggage and in return demanded *baksheesh*, a socially required donation/fee. I was seeing the underbelly of the Indian culture, which I would run into in many different ways, counterbalanced with the serenely beautiful and spiritual side. But looking back, the underbelly of India is small potatoes compared to the

US, where corruption on a massive scale is becoming our commonly known reality.

I have to pause, here in 2016, because I have been distracted and heavily involved emotionally with what is going on with our nation's politics. Suffice it to say, there is a strong stench of incitement of violence going on here. What started as an unbelievably outrageous joke has turned into an actual threat to the security of our country and the world and now, specifically, to an opposing candidate's life. It is August and we're ninety days away from the 2016 election.

It has been a wild ride since Donald Trump came on the scene and brought his reality show to politics. We joked about his orange face, his fake comb-over and tiny hands. This narcissistic, misogynistic, racist, xenophobe has dominated the news every day with a new outrageous comment that would have disqualified anyone else from running for president. We keep thinking the latest "gaffe" will undo him. But he seems to get away with murder, which is truly frightening in light of what he said yesterday. He suggested his Second Amendment people take matters into their own hands should Hillary get elected and appoint her liberal anti-gun judges to the Supreme Court. There is a lot of concern about what this kind of talk will lead to, given the volatility of his supporters. He's now calling Clinton and Obama the "founders" of ISIS. It takes only one unstable person out of the millions who own guns and are influenced by Trump to go off the rails and think they are doing the country a big favor by killing either Clinton or Obama. I'm hoping that whatever unseen forces have protected Obama all these years are also on the job for Hillary.

As the landscape began to light up with the rising sun, we arrived at the ashram* around seven. I dragged my trunk to the place where I was told Swami James stayed, which turned out to be a grass hut with an earthen floor. I peeked in and heard snoring. He was sound asleep, surrounded by a mosquito net, so I quietly went back outside to sit on my trunk and think. I watched other sannyasins silently floating in and out of the complex in long cotton robes as if in a dream. I had on a stylish knee-length red dress, along with high heels and a maroon fake-fur jacket. At this point, I decided to go mainstream and secure a room in a local luxury hotel for at least a week so I could get acclimated. I hailed a rickshaw, which regularly drove by this complex. It took me to the nearest upscale hotel called The Blue Diamond Hotel.

The Osho ashram in Pune, India, is now a first-class commercialized resort, retreat center, and "multiversity," unrecognizable from the Rajneesh ashram I remember in 1981. (Bhagwan changed his name to Osho after leaving Oregon in 1985.)

Here I was in Bhagwan's Holy Land. I could feel his energy all around me (it was like the scent of Jasmine) and couldn't wait to see him in person at his daily two-hour discourse in Buddha Hall. After settling into my hotel room and sleeping for a solid three hours, I got up and hurriedly returned to the commune in something simpler and more appropriate. I registered for some workshops and received a communal introduction/instruction sheet and a schedule from Ma Anand Sheela, Bhagwan's assistant secretary. This is when I found out Bhagwan was in strict quarantine, because someone arrived with chicken pox, and he wouldn't be speaking for a while.

PING! I answered a call from a man named José. Pulling up to the area where he should be, I saw a disheveled Latino sitting on the curb with his head in his hands. I thought to myself, *Oh no, he's a homeless drunk.* Turned out he was very sick, having a reaction to the medication given to him for lupus. He was also an Uber driver, so he had a plastic bag handy in case he vomited, which he thought might happen before we reached his destination: the emergency room at Kaiser. I expressed my sincere concern for him and engaged in a conversation about Uber driving, saying I was writing a book about it, and asked if he had any great stories he could share. This seemed to take his mind off his condition, and

he was excited to relate a couple of stories that he loved. By the time we got to Kaiser, he was feeling much better and smiling. He thanked me for listening and caring. I drove away happy that I didn't allow my initial judgment, which was so completely wrong, take over and prevent me from having the kind of exchange we did. I was glad that I could help this sweet man in his time of need.

It was a full month before Bhagwan came out, and to make matters worse, he went into complete permanent silence. No more discourses and no more darshans (personal dialogues and energy transfers) by him. Drawing from my experience with the Buddhist organization and the victim mentality I'd acquired, I narcissistically believed that it was because I was there.

Well, I was dead-on right. In bringing my victimhood condition to India, I called in an experience that resonated with that mindset. For years as a Buddhist, I felt victimized because I was never promoted to senior leader status and therefore denied access to special meetings with our headquarters chief and others I admired. Now it reflected exactly in the fact that Bhagwan was unavailable to me in the ways he had been to thousands of others for years. Had I come just a month earlier, I would have had a completely different experience. In fact, my friend Krishna Prem at Geetam kept warning me to try and get to India as soon as possible. What did he know, and why didn't I heed his warning? Simple. I was a victim and had to play it out by experiencing it fully. Not being able to hear Bhagwan's discourses nor receive his darshan was the perfect setup for me to continue feeling like a victim.

I signed up for a handful of workshops, which was customary upon entering the commune. The first one, Centering, was three solid days of being asked and asking another only one question: "Who are you?" After listing all the ways I defined myself over and over again, I began to realize I'm none of those things. There was a moment when all preconceived ideas of myself disappeared and I experienced a connection to my heart that was a moment of complete and utter bliss.

Coming out of that blissful state, I happily went to my Gestalt Art workshop, thinking I would be showing off my artistic talent, but instead I was thrown into my prior condition of being a victim through a form of Gestalt therapy. I was then allowed to scream at Bhagwan's portrait on the wall until my rage and self-pity dissolved into a puddle of sweat and tears on the floor.

We were thrown into many exercises involving sexual relatedness. Once, I was put in the center of the room with a young man, and we were told to flirt with each other through only eye contact and sensuous body movements. It was awkward at first, but after some coaching by the facilitator, we ended up in an embrace. Then we were given one piece of letter-sized paper and a child's watercolor set and paintbrush and instructed to paint for the next six hours on that one piece of paper. I was done with my composition in thirty minutes, but no, I had to continue for the next five and a half hours on that same piece of paper. This was an ego-smashing exercise for me, which, despite my sincerely held doubts, yielded acceptable results in the end. I then went home with a complete stranger that night, as ordered, and slept with him in a hammock outdoors. I don't remember how we hooked up: if I initiated it or if he did. Nevertheless, he was a cute, curly-haired Italian who was very respectful and sweet.

We were both kind of shy, this being the first such experience for both of us. We gingerly climbed into the hammock and lay on our backs, cuddling close and looking up at the starry sky. Suddenly, I felt his hot breath on my neck and a hand sliding over my belly and softly brushing my left breast as he brought his hand up to my face, preparing me for a tender kiss. My whole body responded with electricity, and the kiss became a tsunami of passion. I don't remember what happened after that except it was orgasmic. I felt like a wild animal and couldn't get enough. I must have consumed him, because there was little left of him after that, nor me, for that matter. My thirteen years of celibacy became ancient history that night, like dust in the wind. Exhausted, we laughed and scooped up our clothes to cover our bodies as we lay together, blissfully ready for sleep in the softly rocking hammock. The moon winked at us between rustling leaves on the trees above us, and in the distance, a peacock howled its approval.

Bhagwan once said that monogamy was unnatural and intimate relationships should last only a year and a half at most. I don't believe he meant this as a fact but rather as a device to shake up our preconceived ideas on sex, love, and marriage. This may have been good news for his male sannyasins but not for most women, who, the minute they let a man "inside," become attached and strive for a long-term relationship.

Marriage Is Really a Dilemma

"Without marriage there will be no misery—and no laughter either. There will be so much silence . . . it will be Nirvana on the earth! Marriage keeps thousands of things going on: the religion, the state, the nations, the wars, the literature, the movies, the science. Everything, in fact, depends on the institution of marriage. I am not against marriage; I simply want you to be aware that there is a possibility of going beyond it too. But that possibility also opens up only because marriage creates so much misery for you, so much anguish and anxiety for you that you have to learn how to transcend it. It is a great push for transcendence. Marriage is not unnecessary; it is needed to bring you to your senses, to bring you to your sanity. Marriage is necessary and yet there comes a point when you have to transcend it too."

—Bhagwan Shree Rajneesh, *TAO: The Golden Gate*, vol. 2, talk 9

I believe the workshops were designed to smash the illusion of our unconscious dependency on relationships for our happiness. The only commitment that was emphasized by Bhagwan was to one's own awakening (self-love).

"Both males and females must ultimately become androgynous and harmonious sexual beings. They must learn to complete their own circuit of life's energy without sexual union with another and therein, be in resonance with the cosmic, oceanic energy field always present. Then the feelings of sex are transcended; one is in love with all that is."

—**Bhagwan Shree Rajneesh, *The Mustard Seed***

Finally, after one month, Bhagwan made his appearance every morning for music satsang. He was driven in a white Rolls-Royce limo to behind the stage area from which he appeared. He walked slowly to his chair while scanning the room and making eye contact with everyone with a Namaste (hands in prayer) gesture. He then sat and closed his eyes while musicians played enchantingly beautiful flute and sitar music. Our heads were bowed and eyes closed in deep meditation with the music. Once, without thinking, I opened my eyes and saw that Bhagwan was looking straight at me. It was a serendipity moment. Then drums and percussion instruments were added to pick up the beat, and he waved his arms rhythmically to stir up the energy. Many of his musicians went on to become world-renowned New Age instrumentalists, such as Kitaro, Deuter, Deva Premal, and Miten. Music meditations were a central part of the Rajneesh program.

Buddha Hall was a massive white tent with a cement floor accommodating about three thousand people, mostly from India, Europe, Japan, and America We were packed like sardines in kneeling and cross-legged positions on the floor. We had to leave our shoes at the door while an attendant handed us a cough drop. They prohibited any coughing during satsang. You would be escorted out if you coughed. I had a chronic cough from smoking, but I learned very quickly to control it with tears streaming down my cheeks. I was never escorted out.

Bhagwan had devised over sixty-four variations of meditations, many of which involve music and dancing blindfolded. His most famous meditation, practiced daily by everyone, was a one-hour five-part series of movements called Dynamic Meditation, done first thing in the morning. Blindfolded, we begin the first ten minutes doing the "dragon's breath" (pushing the breath out of our noses rapidly with our bellies), which would then move into ten minutes of screaming and pounding the floor with our fists and then ten minutes of jumping up and down with arms over our heads, shouting "Hoo, Hoo, Hoo" from the belly, then to 10 minutes of total silence and standing perfectly still with arms still up in the air, and then to the remaining time of dancing softly to music playing again. This was a very challenging meditation, but it can be life changing if done every day for three weeks (so they say).

My favorite meditation was Vipassana, which was ten days of absolute silence while sitting blindfolded for hours at a time. Every forty-five minutes or so, someone would come up and tap you on the head with a stick to make sure you weren't asleep. In between sittings, you would remove the blindfold and do the Zen walk (picture a movie of someone walking in very slow motion), which was so slow it would take thirty minutes to complete a circle around the relatively small area (a canopied rooftop porch). There was no talking, reading, writing, or even making eye contact with the other participants this whole time. Eating was also done slowly with extreme awareness of every morsel of food being digested. Try it sometime . . . the simplest food will taste like manna from heaven.

One of the greatest things about this meditation is the awareness of life on the outside through the cacophony of recognizable everyday sounds. One such sound came from the stairwell leading to our rooftop, occasionally inhabited by a female who had two or three sexual encounters during those ten days. The lovemaking sounds were impossible to miss. It was a form of extreme discipline to control your teenage urge to giggle.

PING! An attractive young couple in their twenties climbed into the back seat for a thirty-minute ride from Union Square in

San Francisco to Sausalito in Marin. I started chatting with them, but they barely heard me and answered only with "yeah, uh-huh" and then giggled as they seemed to be locked into another agenda. Catching a glimpse of them pawing each other and in a passionate kiss, I turned on the radio to drown out the sounds of foreplay. When I perceived that it was getting out of control, I swerved the car, seeming to avoid an accident, but that didn't work. So then I stopped suddenly while going down a steep hill, which successfully interrupted their little back-seat tryst. Finally, they either got the message or gave up. She smoothed her hair and took out her cosmetic bag to freshen her makeup. He coughed self-consciously while straightening his shirt. They looked back at me in the rearview mirror and smiled sheepishly when our eyes met (so cute). I nodded and said we were almost at their destination and commented on what a lovely day it was. They both responded in unison very enthusiastically, "Oh yes!" and then I heard a muffled giggle as he whispered something in her ear. They acted as if they had succeeded in getting away with something unnoticed by their Uber driver.

Regarding Rajneesh's infamous sex workshops, my experience of them is that they were liberating while being confrontational. As mentioned before, we were often instructed to go home with someone we didn't know and sleep with them and report our insights about it the next day. Mostly, they were exercises in dismantling false beliefs we have about our bodies, and our fears of exposing ourselves to judgment, humiliation, and rejection. The commune's restrooms had open stalls used by both men and women. It took some getting used to, but eventually, you thought nothing of it.

It amuses me that while I write this, there are people in government who are so uptight about the transgender bathroom issue that they are trying to pass laws to discriminate against them. They believe this will protect the privacy of everyone else. Bhagwan was way ahead of his time and apparently still is.

I got used to riding my bike everywhere except to downtown Pune, when I would take a motorized rickshaw or hitch a ride on the back of a motor scooter. I lived in a complex of four separate huts situated behind a mansion owned by a freethinking Indian princess who loved sannyasins. Apparently, sometime in the past, she went against her father's wishes for an arranged marriage to a raja (nobleman) and was disowned by her family.

My hut had cement floors and walls and an outdoor shower with cold water (perfect for summer weather). Every morning, I awoke beneath my mosquito net to the crowing of peacocks and the call to prayer by a Hindu male singer over a loudspeaker in the distance.

Most everyone in my neighboring huts were Italian, and they often liked to party at night outside in our shared patio, dancing to many amateur players of drums and flutes. The princess always liked to come to our parties. She invited me for tea in her mansion a few times. She was elegant and beautiful and spoke perfect English.

During my time in India, I had two or three phone calls from my mother, checking up on me to make sure I was OK. Looking back, it never even occurred to me to call Dad or expect a call from him. He more or less faded from my life when I became a sannyasin. I think he felt betrayed, knowing that I had given Bhagwan the unconditional love and respect generally accorded a father. Later, when I returned and confronted him, he confessed that he didn't love me anymore and instead was compelled to focus all his love and attention on my adopted brother. At the time I was shocked and deeply wounded. But now, writing this, it all makes sense. He was the one who was wounded. He had invested his whole life in my success and well-being: caring for me as a doctor-father when I was sick; giving me piano lessons, art lessons, and singing lessons; coaching me as a performer; and then sending me off to college. He was particularly proud of my success in the TV industry and bragged about me to all his friends. The thanks I gave him was chucking my successful career and running off to India to be with some "fast-talking guru."

In between workshops, my new sannyasin friends and I often got together to either go sunbathing and swimming in the nude at the local well (a deep fifteen-foot-wide cement hole with an eighteen-foot ladder to the water) or go shopping in the town of Pune. Once, while waiting for a rickshaw, I saw a group of Indian men and women (not sannyasins) walking toward me with a baby girl. Pointing to her, they motioned very excitedly. "You take? Only five hundred rupees, please." I was nonplussed. I didn't know it was sometimes customary for families to sell their youngest daughters. They didn't look like beggars or paupers. They were very nicely dressed, the men in business suits and the women in silk saris, and the beautiful baby girl sported a gold earring.

Another time in downtown Pune, while shopping at a small souvenir store, an elderly Indian man dressed in white with a white turban was sitting cross-legged on the counter. He suddenly grabbed my arm, saying, "I am very good guru. You come. Be my disciple." Right away I showed him my mala with Bhagwan's picture. He scowled and brushed it aside as if to say I had made a very poor choice.

Shopping in Pune was uniquely interesting, with "sacred" cows (all cows are sacred according to the Hindu religion in India) lounging in small street corridors, where you dare not touch them or bother them in any way. Sometimes, you'd see a procession of people singing and playing flutes and tambourines along with a brightly decorated elephant carrying a fringed canopy, beneath which a bride and groom majestically sat. And, of course, there were beggars everywhere and children following you asking for *baksheesh*. Now, with all the homeless in America, we are not far behind this sad scenario.

Being that he was outrageously controversial, breaking all the rules for a spiritual guru by embracing material wealth and free sex, it was no wonder Rajneesh was not very well liked in the Indian community, and therefore, neither were his sannyasins. Once, while I was riding my bike, a local deliberately ran into me with his bike, and I ended up flat on the ground with my bike on top of me. No one offered to help me up. They just stood there and nudged each other, laughing. We stood out because of our red clothing. Sannyasins of other "more legitimate" gurus traditionally wore only saffron-colored robes and then only after many years of devotion to their guru and his teachings. Rajneesh was considered a renegade guru in India. He left India eventually because the government didn't recognize his as a legitimate religion and decided that he owed them ten million dollars in back taxes.

Speaking of which, I was in the middle of my third month in Pune and was shopping downtown when I had a sudden panicky urge to return to the commune as soon as possible. I hailed a rickshaw and, when I arrived, found out that Bhagwan had just left for America secretively with a small group of his disciples.

Again, I felt betrayed. I sat on the curb and thought, *What am I going to do now?* I had come to India to live forever with Bhagwan. It felt like I had been punched in the stomach. Now everything seemed hollow and meaningless. Others joined me, and we all hugged each other in our shared emptiness. We had heard something like this was going to happen. There were secret preparations made, but nothing was ever announced and no timeline was publicly known. We all got up and walked aimlessly to nowhere in particular, deep in thought. During this moment, I acquired a young male companion, Swami Prem Deva, who held my hand and invited me to have chai with him to talk over possibilities. I welcomed this new wrinkle in my massively wrinkled journey.

As he proved no threat to my longstanding fear of commitment, we decided to move in together in a new space to figure things out for ourselves individually, using each other for support. I went looking on my own for the ideal apartment. I was told that there was a certain swami (all male sannyasins were called *swami* and women *ma*) who had real estate connections, and they gave me his address. Knocking on his door, I was greeted by an Indian butler who directed me to a bedroom down the hall. By this time nothing much surprised or shocked me, but I was totally unprepared for what I encountered that day: an unabashedly handsome semi-naked European or American man between two beautiful naked women in a threesome embrace on a king-size bed. Of course, I acted as though nothing was out of the ordinary and continued to inquire about an apartment.

PING! Arriving at a cute cottage in San Anselmo, I rang the passenger up after waiting two minutes. A woman named Aggie answered, laughing, "Oh, I'm in the middle of making love to a complete stranger. I'll be down in a minute." I couldn't believe what I'd just heard and thought I must have heard it wrong. Down came a nice-looking guy with short brown hair and beard and a baseball hat, carrying a woman's bag and shoes. He climbed in, saying she'd be down soon.

We waited another five to seven minutes, then finally, slowly, stumbling barefoot down the stairs, came a rather plain, heavyset, long-haired hippie in her early forties, wearing a long cotton lavender-print dress. To my mind, this was not a match, but apparently I'm not a very good judge of that, as he was totally into her. They smooched in the back seat as I proceeded to their destination.

She was drunk and very talkative, shouting out many times, "Where's my keys? Oh, here they are!" followed by gales of laughter. She decided to brag about her sister, who was currently working on a thriller movie in New York as the prop master. I brightened up, thinking I could join in the conversation by saying I had also worked in the business, but was brusquely ignored, as I had interrupted her important stream of thought. I remained quiet the rest of the ride. Her friend seemed to be quite taken with her story. She finally put her shoes on and found her keys, and they departed, he with his arm around her waist holding her firm, as she was quite unsteady and still talking and laughing loudly.

Why is it that a very plain, overweight, and ridiculous-acting

woman has no trouble finding love? Why am I still so unlucky in this area? Is it perhaps because I am still overly judgmental? Hmmmm!

Prem Deva and I stayed together for the next month or so in a large one-bedroom apartment and played house. We experienced the famous Indian monsoon, which was preceded by swarms of mosquitos and millions of little frogs everywhere. The mosquitos were particularly bothersome while trying to ride a bike. You would have to have at least one hand, and sometimes two, batting them away or shielding your eyes. Young Indian women love the monsoon. They celebrate by dancing wildly in the street while getting drenched. It always follows a very hot summer, and the rain is a welcome relief.

13

UP, UP, AND AWAY
To Unchartered Territory

After my brief affair with this sweet, young pretend husband, I, and many sannyasins, made arrangements to go to Amsterdam for the 1981 Orange Affair Festival, called "The Last Tango in Poona," before returning home. A month before leaving, I had engaged an Indian tailor to sew a halter-top party dress with three yards of fancy dress fabric I bought. It was a simple design that I drew on paper. It took all of four weeks for him to complete the job. I went back every week in hopes it would be finished, but he always had some reason why it wasn't and would assure me that it would be finished next week. Finally, the fourth week, with fingers crossed, I knocked on his door just hours before my plane was scheduled to depart for Bombay, where I would then fly to Amsterdam. He still hadn't finished it, and I explained in a rather loud voice that he must finish it then and there because I was leaving. He sat me down in the living room and had his wife prepare a delicious meal while I waited. An hour later, he presented me with the finished product, which was unfortunately pretty shoddy. Apparently, that design was completely unfamiliar to him and hard for him to translate into an actual garment. I thanked him anyway and pretended that it was perfect. I hurriedly left and threw it in a public trashcan before hailing a rickshaw.

Our Amsterdam adventure began with a harrowing experience on a flight from Bombay. Just after takeoff, I looked out my window and saw that one of the engines was on fire. An announcement came over the loudspeaker saying that we were circling Bombay and dumping fuel from that engine into the Indian Ocean before landing back in Bombay. "*Om mani padme Om!*" There were a lot of incantations and chanting in the cabin while we circled. We landed safely and were treated to a luxury hotel on the beach for two days. This was the first time I'd had a hot bath in over three months. I felt like the queen of Sheba while I lathered up in a warm bath full of scented bubbles. We were treated like royalty, with beautiful banquets of food laid out for us in addition to prompt service to our rooms for anything we needed or wanted. I hooked up with a tall, good-looking German swami who didn't speak a word of English—or I German. But somehow, we got along just fine (smile).

Two days later, floating on a cloud (and scrubbed clean), we headed back to the airport. Cheerfully, we gathered around a sannyasin guitarist and sang some of our Rajneesh songs waiting to board our new plane. What happened next stopped us in our tracks! Picture a group of happy, excited people rushing to get on board after being called and suddenly coming to a dead stop, bumping into each other as they all see that the new plane is, in fact, the original plane, but *now a new engine is strapped onto the wing with chains next to the old burned-out engine!*

Dear Mother of God! What do we do now? I had forgotten this was India, and this is what you call a *jugaad* solution. In India, *jugaad* means "hack." This Indian philosophy means getting the job done, no matter how sloppy or inefficient, but always with flair and a sales pitch. I experienced this often in Pune; when going to buy a dress, I was always met with a bobbing head that said, "Very fine quality, madam," even if a seam was ripped or buttons hung by a thread. I laugh about it now, but at that particular moment, it was no laughing matter as we wondered if this would be our last day on Planet Earth. Again, chanting and incantations sprung up everywhere, but miraculously the fix got us to Holland safely.

Thousands of us descended upon the Amsterdam canals, ending up at a large hall, dancing, singing, eating, attending lectures, and then sleeping in a rented and abandoned prison. Our first night, after the day's events, we slept huddled together on cold concrete floors in a jail cell, and the next night I found a bunk bed in a hostel for a lot more comfort and sleep. Both were quite a departure from the luxury hotel we were treated to in Bombay.

Coming back to the States was a shock to my nervous system after three months of meditation, gentle group love, and joyous celebration. It's as if I was suddenly thrown into a world of sharp elbows and migraine headaches. I found that my costumers union membership had lapsed, so I was now a low-level Costumer 1 again, looking for work in the movie and TV industry. I ended up doing a lot of TV commercials, which were one or two-day assignments. I also did a couple of days on the TV version of *10* with Bo Derrick, Dudley Moore, and Julie Andrews. It turned out to be mostly the naked pool scene with a porn group from San Francisco. I had little work to do as the wardrobe coordinator, except to provide towels. Poor Dudley had to come out to the pool area in full frontal to the unbridled snickers of cast and crew. But he was such a good sport he laughed roundly when someone cracked a joke about the size of his "humble appendage." Meanwhile, members of the porn group hung out everywhere in provocative poses in between takes in broad daylight. It was unnerving even to this prior jetsetter and seasoned Rajneesh disciple.

About two months later, Sandesh and Daya, a couple of very enterprising sannyasins I met in India, invited me to live with them in the Monkees' old house in Laurel Canyon. My stepbrother, Les, and my Buddhist friend (*Dallas* actor) Patrick Duffy helped me move from my apartment to what later became the infamous Rajneesh

Hollywood house. This cut down my living expenses to a fraction of what I was paying before, as I shared this space with nine other full-time residents. It was a huge house with many levels. The garage was converted into two bedrooms accommodating four, and the sunporch also housed four people, usually guests. We had guests coming and going from around the world all the time, so full capacity reached eighteen at one point.

Apart from my time in a sorority at Berkeley and a dorm at UCLA, this was my first experience in communal living. While in India I shared a space with only one other person. The Pune ashram was essentially a meeting place: Buddha Hall, a building for dozens of workshops, a cafeteria, administrative offices, bookstore, arts and crafts shop, mind/body treatment and medical center, publishing house, and living quarters for Bhagwan and key staff members.

PING! **Coming from a ranch-style home in Marin was a short dark-haired woman of unknown nationality until we engaged in a conversation. I found out her name, Aruna, meant "clear and bright like the sun," and she was an au pair from Mongolia who was studying to be an accountant in San Francisco. I asked her where Mongolia was, not being well versed in global geography, and she said it was near China. I then asked how it compared to her experience in the US, and she became effusive in her appreciation of our country due to the fact that at the age of fifty, she would be considered old and useless in her country, with no possibility for employment. She reported that her parents died shortly after they turned fifty, and she swore that would never happen to her. I told her my age, and her eyes got big and she gasped, saying, "Wow, you are certainly proof of the American dream." She then laughingly said her favorite pastime was swinging on the monkey bars in the park near her home, which she did every day to the amazement of passersby. I applauded this woman who escaped the death sentence her country would have given her.**

We took turns keeping our Monkees house clean, cooking dinner, and washing dishes. It was efficient and fun. I became a vegetarian and was amazed at the great variety of gourmet vegetarian dishes many of the girls knew how to cook. Besides eating sumptuous meals, dishwashing was the most fun, done to Flashdance's "What a Feeling," Bee Gees' "Stayin' Alive," The Beatles, and other pop stars of the seventies and eighties. We didn't have a TV for entertainment, just weed, wine, and each other. We often sat around the fireplace sipping wine and sharing a joint and talking about what we were going to do when we got to the ranch where Bhagwan had settled in Oregon. Most of the residents were from England or Germany, with a few of us "Westerners" in the mix.

Contrary to what you might think went on at that house, we never had any orgies, and everyone was very discreet about their sex life. The so-called orgies in Pune were therapeutic workshops done with the written consent of all participants for the purpose of releasing unhealthy notions of sex and discovering our own authentic and natural sexuality. Bhagwan was way ahead of his time and, of course, vilified constantly by the local press and Indian government. Years later, I saw a documentary about the ashram in Pune made in the US, and it was manifestly incorrect and sensationalized with its portrayal of communal sex orgies.

One thing we did at the Hollywood house, which might've lapsed into an orgy had we not been so respectful of each other, was our Wednesday night group massage. We would assemble in groups of five, with one person lying on the floor in the middle while the other four worked on his/her torso, arms, hands, feet, and head. We would alternate every thirty minutes so that everyone got a thirty-minute massage. It was a meditative, albeit sensual, experience with scented candles, a flickering fire in the fireplace, and soft music flooding the darkened room. What happened later in the privacy of the bedrooms of already formed couples can be left to your imagination.

Every day in this house was an adventure, with very little conflict. I loved everyone for the unique and loving individuals they were. There were no blanket belief systems, as with the Buddhist group I was married to before. We enjoyed our diversity and our universal intelligence. Our love of Bhagwan, along with meditation and celebration, was our common bond.

Now that Rajneesh had relocated to the US, intermarriages began popping up between American and European sannyasins so they could live legally with their spouses on the ranch in Oregon.

I agreed to marry Tosh, a Brit, for whom I had a schoolgirl crush. Naively, I thought this would give me an opening to his heart. He was a professional actor from London and had been in charge of the drama group in Pune. He was also assigned to protect Bhagwan and lived in his compound as a trained samurai (sannyasins who had black belts from the West). Being the crass opportunist I was, I also calculated that marrying him would give me a free ticket to be among the hierarchy at Rajneeshpuram, the ranch in Oregon, where we were all preparing to move.

PING! **As I write this, something very interesting is happening in my world of Uber. The other day, Nate, a handsome young Jewish man (late twenties or early thirties) almost seemed to be hitting on me. When I picked him up, he was very friendly and commented that he was really appreciative of my picking him up. We were engaged in small talk, and I noticed in my rearview mirror he was looking at me with a look I remembered from men years ago, when he suddenly asked if I was married. No one had asked me that question in at least twelve years. Embarrassed, I mumbled, "No, you?"**

He said, "Me neither." Long pause, and then he asked, "What do you do for fun?"

I purposely ignored the ramifications of this conversation and answered honestly, "Not much, just dance Sunday mornings at Sweat Your Prayers in Sausalito."

He said, "Oh, my old girlfriend used to do that too."

Deciding to meet him head-on but in a humorous way, I said, "Old? How old? Surely not as old as me?"

He laughed and said, "Oh no, that's not what I meant." With that, we both laughed, and there were no more innuendos. But when he left, he gave me a ten-dollar tip, which I tried to refuse. He smiled and said, "Please take it. I really enjoyed talking to you."

A much darker version of this situation happened when I pulled up to a sprawling ranch-style house where two men were holding up a third, whom they poured into my front passenger seat. The guy (I forgot his name) was unintelligible except for the fact that he apparently thought I was a twenty-something chick and started blatantly hitting on me. The time it took to drive to his house seemed like an eternity as I fended off the advances of this deaf, dumb, and blindly drunk man. He was deaf because he obviously didn't hear me say "NO!"; dumb because great amounts of alcohol do that to you; and blind because, as good as my genes are, I'm obviously well over twenty years of age.

Tosh held court every morning in the breakfast room with his gorgeous good looks and engaging wit. I've always been attracted to comedians, especially handsome ones, and Tosh had it all. Unfortunately, I had little of what he wanted, except access to a green card. His attention was on someone else in our house. Not knowing that, I felt really lucky to have this opportunity to get to know him on a more intimate level. Tosh was an actor, and I was still involved with the studios, so he asked if I would help him with a scene he was rehearsing for an audition. We spent a few nights going over his lines and getting to know each other better. This didn't help me as much as it did him. I was falling, and he was taking advantage of that. I was in denial of the fact that all he really wanted from me was a green card.

Preparing for our post-marriage INS interview, we rehearsed our lines and had our pictures taken together, pretending for the camera that we were in love. (He might've been acting, but I wasn't. I was smitten.) We took a trip to my dad's in Fallbrook to introduce him to my new fiancé. Tosh was such a good actor he convinced my dad that he was in love with me (and for a moment, I believed him too), and so Dad approved. We then caravanned to Las Vegas with a few of our friends, found an all-night chapel to take our vows, and stayed overnight at a friend's house, in SEPARATE rooms. It was then that reality bit me in the butt. My dream was shattered when I realized I was just a pawn in Tosh's dream. It really hit home when we came back to the Monkees house and the first thing Tosh did was seek out another woman, a ditzy blond sannyasin beauty (the one he had previously been attracted to), to go to bed with that night

Later, after passing muster with the INS, he obligingly kissed me on the cheek and thanked me for his green card.

I processed my deep, dark disappointment with a fellow female housemate and a "shroom" (magic mushroom). I remember lying on my back alongside my friend on a mushroom high with our four feet propped up on a tree trunk next to the swimming pool. Suddenly she started moaning and writhing ecstatically as though being made love to, and I, in my bitter darkness, said, quite forcefully, "Move over, bitch!" We both broke up in unending peals of laughter, and I was cured right then and there of my romantic fantasy as the shroom laughter let the air out of my billowy heart-shaped balloon.

Earlier this year, I learned of his death, which hit me pretty hard. The woman he married after me, and also divorced, found him alone in his London flat sitting upright in his easy chair. I cried for days after learning of his death. We had a deep connection even though we never became intimate. We were uncannily alike in so many ways, being only one day apart on our Piscean birth charts. It turns out the woman who found him and I have become close friends due to an accidental meeting twelve years ago when I registered for one of her workshops, not knowing she was the ditzy blond beauty who had stolen my honeymoon. My perception of her changed radically after meeting her a second time: she literally changed my life with her profoundly powerful and insightful three-day women's workshop called "Celebration of Being." She is my dear friend Rajyo, and ditzy she is NOT.

Coming back to the Monkees house: word got out at the ranch that the Hollywood bunch were rebellious toward the ranch because of Ma Anand Sheela, who willfully replaced and threw out Laxmi, Bhagwan's beloved, longstanding secretary from Pune. Ma Lakshmi visited our house for a couple of days, and I was amazed that such a powerful woman, vilified by Sheela, could be so petite and gentle and sweet. Another gentleman that visited us on occasion was the one-and-only Pune real estate stud who operated from his king-size office bed surrounded by beautiful naked women. He had charm oozing out of his pores, but he was genuinely open and loving toward everyone. He was appropriately known as the "Lovebaba," and he later became the ranch disc jockey for our very own nightclub. Ma Anand Sheela was usually addressed by everyone as Sheela.

Finally, we all made arrangements to arrive at the ranch a few days before the first world festival there that summer. We made slanderous T-shirt slogans expressing our antipathy toward Ma Anand Sheela and Co., but once we got there, I don't believe any of us wore them.

Prior to leaving, we had a party with just the house residents to celebrate our departure. I took all the women to Frederick's of Hollywood and maxed out my credit card, buying outrageous outfits to wear to our party. We also bought several cans of Reddi Wip. It was a wild night and probably the closest we ever came to an orgy. We paraded before the guys in our scanty sequined and plumed costumes and quite naturally proceeded to do a strip tease to joyous whoops and hollers. This segued into energetic dancing by all to loud disco music. The night ended with two scantily clothed women covered in Reddi Wip, which was brazenly licked off by everyone else. Sorry . . .

but that was the extent of our orgy. Nothing else happened, except we lay around, mellow on weed, snuggling together on the floor and the big comfy couch, exhausted from all the laughter and the night's raucous high energy. One by one, as the fire in the fireplace died down, we peeled off and went to our respective rooms to sleep the rest of the night away.

At this point in my life, communal living was the best of all scenarios for my growth. Prior to Buddhism and after college, I was primarily a loner and not much of a partygoer. With Buddhism, I came out of my cave and was socially connected to a large group of people every day. I did form some lasting friendships that are still ongoing, but most others were superficial in comparison to the relationships formed through close day-to-day living circumstances.

In communal living, you learn so much more about yourself in relation to your housemates. You see the good, the bad, and the ugly, and you move through it. There is no hiding, no posturing, and no illusions of grandeur or victimhood. I think the meditation helped too. It's like a marriage, but what was perfect for me is that I was not bound to one person day in and day out. I had choices every day to be with whomever I wanted to hang with or relate to. My anathema to a traditional marriage is symptomatic of the influences in my life growing up as a typical sensitive Piscean around demonstrably unaffectionate parents.

PING! PING! **This is called a pool pickup, where more than one rider shares a ride coming from the same basic location and ending in nearly the same location, each of them saving money. One girl with honey-blond hair in a long braid and bright blue eyes sat in the front with me, and then I picked up another, whom I will call Nefertiti, a stunning black woman with Egyptian-styled hair, who sat in the back. Honey-Blond had just graduated from UCLA and was working in the environmental field, and Nefertiti was a dance teacher of Gabrielle Roth's Five Rhythms.**

The ride was long enough to get to know these two beautiful women, and our conversation veered off to my experience in India and being with Bhagwan, to which Nefertiti slapped the back of my seat in disbelief. She exclaimed that she was a devoted fan and read passages from his books to her dance students every day. She wanted to know what it was like to be in his presence.

She had never met anyone who had known him and was hungry to know more. Honey-Blond was drawn into the conversation, which was highly charged and giddy with happy camaraderie. As she was leaving, she said this was the best Uber ride she'd ever had. Right away Nefertiti moved up to the front seat, asking more questions. I told her we should get together sometime when there was more time, since there was so much to talk about. We agreed and exchanged emails. I saw in her the essence of a high priestess.

14

I FEEL THE EARTH MOVE
It's a Seismic Awakening!

About ten thousand sannyasins from around the world descended upon the ranch at the First Annual World Festival in 1982. My group boarded a ranch school bus that came to pick us up at the airport in Redmond, Oregon. We had a bumpy ride on the narrow road to the ranch, which took thirty minutes from the main road. The whole property consisted of sixty-four thousand acres of desert in Central Oregon. The first thing we had to do when we entered the "city" was pass a lice and crab examination before being admitted to our housing, which consisted of randomly assigned tents for four on wooden platforms.

In the eight months prior to our arrival, a lot of work had been accomplished, with clean water and electricity, three thousand tents on platforms, many group bathroom and shower buildings strategically placed, new dirt roads, a huge structure for Buddha Hall and several manufactured buildings for offices, a large cafeteria, bookstore, dairy and chicken farm, and a hydroponic garden.

At the actual festivities in Buddha Hall, we finally saw our beloved Bhagwan as he drove slowly on the road lined with cheering sannyasins around the gigantic structure in his white Rolls-Royce limousine. All ten thousand of us scampered back into the great hall and took part in the ecstatic experience of meditating and then dancing together to the music and waves of energy conducted by Bhagwan's graceful hands. I was in a trance from the sheer ecstasy of all the love generated by him and ten thousand sannyasins.

Immediately afterward, while leaving Buddha Hall, I was accosted by a TV camera while a microphone was shoved into my face by a Ken-doll anomaly called a news anchorman, who asked how I felt and why. All I could say was "Love is everything." Later, I chastised myself for such a stupid remark and for missing such a great opportunity to be articulate for my master. I just now randomly opened Bhagwan's book *Ancient Music in the Pines* to page 143. He sometimes sends me messages this way.

"Then by and by, if you relax, and if you are not too much worried about your image in the eyes of others, your own authentic face, your original face, comes into being—the face that you had before you were born, and the face that you will again have when you are dead, the original face, not the cultivated mask. With that original face you will see God everywhere, because with the original face you can meet with the original, with the reality."

Back in California, we returned to our ordinary lives. Some were making plans to return by the next year to live and work at the ranch, while others, my husband included, would have none of it as long as Sheela was in charge.

Members of the ranch's inner circle, Hasya (who later replaced Sheela as Bhagwan's secretary) and her close friend Kaveesha, along with two other millionaire sannyasins, David and Dyan John, moved into a huge mansion close by our house in Hollywood. Their primary purpose was to bring Bhagwan's meditations and teachings to elite Southern California society by creating weeklong spiritual retreats replete with all the luxury of a European spa hotel. Hasya was the former wife of a famous Oscar-winning movie producer, so she had all the connections. They commissioned me to design maroon robes to be worn by the guests. My housemate Daya, a seamstress and an ex-London model, helped me create and put them together. I don't think the project lasted beyond the first two or three groups, but it seemed like a great idea at the time. We occasionally went there to hang out with them, as they were really beautiful, fun-loving people.

One time, myself and two other sannyasins from our house decided to drive up to the ranch in my Honda and pay a visit, but we got only as far as the other side of the Grapevine (a long steep hill outside of LA on Hwy. 5) when I let one of them take over the wheel. We were speeding along at seventy-five miles per hour when suddenly she swerved, and the car careened over the side and rolled three times, blowing out all the windows and tires. The three of us sustained bruises and cracked ribs. This was perhaps my second out-of-body experience, because I remember watching the car roll over while I didn't; I was just hanging there in space while everything swirled around me.

We were taken to the nearby hospital for X-rays and first aid and then sent home on a bus. My car was totaled and left for pickup by a junkyard. Just two months prior, I had let my insurance lapse. Still playing the victim, I meekly asked for some appropriate compensation by the driver who totaled my car. She was independently wealthy but felt she should give me only $150. (She was in her power; I wasn't.) So, I was left without a car for several months, trying to find work by walking and taking buses from Santa Monica to LA, which is a daunting task. It was a tough time, but somehow I made it through to the next summer festival at the ranch. While there, I was asked to stay and work as a gas station attendant first and later as a truck driver delivering building materials. On the ranch all the jobs were assigned and rotated according to the needs of the commune, not necessarily according to one's abilities or experience.

PING! It was late afternoon in San Rafael, and I picked up Chuck, a thirty-something guy who had had a few beers and was

loose after a hard day's work loading trucks with smelly garbage gathered from the yards of uncared-for homes. Apparently, there are quite a few homeowners who are so unconscious they throw their garbage out un-bagged on their floors and in their yards, enough to keep this guy employed, he surmised, for another five years. Thankfully, he didn't smell like his job. During our thirty-minute drive to Sonoma, he talked incessantly about the woman who was his "queen." He said he was reluctant to propose to her even though they had lived together for years, because he felt completely unworthy of her. "Look at me! What am I but a stupid garbage man? I can't possibly give her what she deserves."

My philanthropic instincts were ignited. "Hey, stop that. She's damn lucky to have someone like you adore her and care for her the best he can. And you're damn lucky to have the love of this woman in your life. How many people can say that? I can't. I don't have anyone but myself." It was a hard sell, but I think I got through to him by the time we landed, and he handed me a crisp ten-dollar bill as a tip.

At last I was in heaven with my beloved Bhagwan and thousands of group-hugging sannyasins! And, oh my God, how the ranch had grown! It now had a beautiful reservoir they called Krishnamurti Lake, which they made by building a huge earthen dam over the creek and importing fine sand for the beach. The preexisting ranch house was remade into a Japanese-style restaurant with American gourmet food. I don't remember all the buildings that were in place when I first arrived in 1982, but when I left three years later, we had a two-story mall called "Zarathustra" with executive offices upstairs and a restaurant, bookstore, ice cream parlor, beauty salon, travel agency, and boutique downstairs. There were separate buildings for a larger boutique with racks of stylish red clothing and accessories, a post office, a discotheque, a hospital, an airport, a garage and machine shop, a gas station, a water filtration plant, a recycling center for building materials, a poultry and dairy farm, a truck farm for our organic fruits and vegetables, a bee farm, a huge cafeteria, a five-star hotel, hundreds of townhomes housing eighteen sannyasins each, another couple of hundred A-frames accommodating two people each, and eighty-five yellow school buses for our public transportation system. Each structure was a work site and was called a "temple." Our work was our meditation.

"Rajneeshpuram exemplifies both the best and the worst of modern cult phenomenon. The collective activity of the commune residents gave rise to the greatest intentional community experiment the modern age has seen. In an article in the New Yorker, journalist Frances Fitzgerald detailed some of the accomplishments the commune had managed by 1983: cleared and planted 3,000 acres of land, built a 350-million-gallon reservoir and fourteen irrigation systems, created a truck farm that provided 90% of the vegetables needed to feed that ranch, a poultry and dairy farm to provide milk and eggs, a 10-megawatt power substation, an 85-bus public transportation system, an urban-use sewer system, a state-of-the-art telephone and computer communications center and 250,000 sq. feet of residential space."

—from *The Rise and Fall of Rajneeshpuram* by Sven Davisson

Except for the article from which I took the above paragraph, most reports mentioned in Google are about the scandals perpetrated by Secretary Sheela—at first, in defiance of the local and state governments and later in pursuit of power for herself. Not much was said about the gargantuan feat of building a fully functional, beautiful, and ahead-of-its-time city with our bare hands. There was nothing about the fact that 67 percent of the residents were college graduates, nearly half of those with doctorate degrees. No, according to some reports, we were all fools brainwashed by Bhagwan.

Interestingly, to some wise pundits, that would be a good thing, meaning we would be clearing our minds of all our preconceived ideas based on fear and self-loathing. Of course, the media thought of it in another way. At that time everyone was concerned that we would be another Jonestown, where the mass suicide of 918 devotees had been ordered and carried out just a few years before. Coincidentally, the daughter of the senator who was assassinated in Jonestown (Senator Joseph Ryan) was a sannyasin who lived at the ranch.

But before I get into the political drama that was occurring under our noses but out of our collective consciousness until it was too blatantly obvious to miss, I'd like to summarize my experience on the ranch as one of the "elite" worker bees. (Yes, this is an oxymoron.)

My first five months there, I lived in a tent with one other, a male sannyasin I didn't know. We hardly ever spoke, because when I came home from work at night, he would be deep in meditation and then go to sleep. We had to get up at dawn and rush to get breakfast before being assigned to our work. Flashlights were a necessity for our shower and bathroom trips at night and early morning, going down a long, winding dirt path to the closest facility. I had brought a bottle of Bailey's Irish Cream as part of my necessities, which I used to reward myself at the end of every day with a hearty sip. That was my preferred meditation. The last month in the tent (November) I would awaken every morning with a sheet of ice on my sleeping bag. Being a native southern Californian, this kind of weather was completely foreign to me.

The first three months or so, I worked as a gas station attendant at the far end of the ranch, near Krishnamurti Lake, learning how to check all the fluids, change the oil, and check the tires of all the trucks on the ranch. I loved this job with my two male attendants, even though one of them never bothered to work but instead spent his time carving beautiful wood sculptures behind the shed. This got to me a little, especially when Bhagwan drove by and stopped to acknowledge Swami Wood Carver while he handed the sculpture of a dove directly to Bhagwan himself.

Coming from thirteen years of Buddhism, where I mastered being a good follower and doing my best at whatever job I was given without complaining, I was unable to express my anger at the unfairness of the situation. And so it festered beneath the surface, building upon my already well-cooked victimhood.

PING! **A handsome young couple piled into the back seat, and right away a lively conversation ensued. The guy seemed to want me to know how positive and creative he was by announcing the fact many times. "I'm a really positive guy . . . I see all the good things in people. Also, I'm an artist!" whereupon he showed me a sculpture on his iPhone that he had on exhibit at the county fair. He proudly explained all the details of this unique bronze wire sculpture of a guitar. His girlfriend was backing up his statements and commending his great talent as an artist and carpenter and as a boyfriend, reiterating it over and over again. (I think they both might have been a little high.) I told him he had a great champion in her. He then turned his attention toward me and said he could read my aura, which, according to him, was bluish green, and then he exclaimed what a wonderful woman I was. But the statement that got me was when he said that I had uplifted him and made him happier than before he entered my car. I blurted out, "But I haven't done anything!" to which he countered, "You don't have to. You just being you with your beautiful energy makes me happy." What is so amazing is that it corresponded exactly with my intentional prayer before driving that day. When I finally dropped them off, he said, "I have to give you a hug," and then he got out and walked around to my door, and we hugged. His girlfriend also wanted a hug. It was a perfect way to begin my day.**

Finally, the day came when we were all assigned a townhouse, which were manufactured two-story homes with nine bedrooms accommodating a total of eighteen sannyasins. There were token living rooms with one chair, a washroom with a washer and dryer for our muddy clothes, and four bathrooms. There was not much social-izing in the townhouses. They were merely sleeping and personal hygiene quarters. All socializing was done on the job or during meal-times. We worked from 7 a.m. to 6 p.m., with a sixty-minute break at Magdalena Cafeteria for lunch and two fifteen-minute breaks where they would hand out snacks to munch on at the jobsite. Depending on where you worked, five minutes by bus or twenty minutes walking were subtracted out of your eating and rest time. At the gas station we were not supervised, so it was a little more lax, and we usually had our own truck to take us to Magdalena (cafeteria). For dinner we could either eat for free at Magdalena or pay for a more elaborate meal at one of our two restaurants. At one point we were awarded coupons that had an allotment of so many boxes per month to mark off for free goodies from the restaurants, ice cream parlor, hair salon, bookstore, or boutiques.

Bhagwan's "drive-by" was an additional break in our day, usually around 2 p.m. Like clockwork, the sannyasins would line up along the road from Bhagwan's house to the center of town, and he would come slowly driving by with his companion Vivek in the front seat of one of his ninety-three Rolls-Royces. Every day he made eye contact with each one of us and gave us a one-handed Namaste. This, more than our lunch, filled us up with great energy for the rest of the day.

One day after about four months at the gas station, I was called into the office and given another job: to drive a pickup truck for the pipe crew. That meant I would drive from one construction site to another with a load of PVC pipes. I loved this job too. My CB moniker was Kundalini Ma, because the truck was so old and bumpy that it could have made my Kundalini rise. Being with all those cute Italians on the pipe crew and sitting with them at lunch was an ego boost. Before that, I didn't know many other sannyasins, and it was stressful to find a table where I felt comfortable and accepted. Very few of the san-nyasins I lived with in Hollywood came to the ranch, except during our yearly world festivals. So I was alone in a sea of red, trying to connect individually or break into already formed sannyasin cliques. Eventually that all changed, and I found myself locked in spontaneous hugging groups every day while hanging out at the mall or walking from one building to another. I also had the advantage of having my own form of transportation and got to know sannyasins by being able to pick them up if they needed a ride while I was en route. (Do you see a connection here?)

As a truck driver, I later branched out to delivering wood, nails, and other building supplies to every building project on the ranch, which included about twelve different sites. Just before the Second Annual World Celebration was to take place, we were redirected to other jobs to accommodate ten to twenty thousand more sannyasins. I ended up on the grounds beautification team, where we simply moved small boulders in a creative way in the urban A-frame area. It was summer, so the heat soared to 118 degrees, with few or no trees to provide shade for relief. Work was very slow and painful, but we survived.

After the festival, which was a joyous occasion seeing old friends from home, I was called into the office once again and given a new assignment: cleaning townhouses, alternating every week with working in the kitchens of all the restaurants, including the one in Antelope called Zorba the Buddha Café. My glorious truck-driving days were over. Now it was just me and toilet bowls and showers, mopping and vacuuming and washing piles of clothes alone in three townhomes every day. I always looked forward to my alternate week at the restaurants.

During all this time I was aware that almost all my friends had been awarded a brass bead, which meant they had been given permanent membership to the commune and didn't have to pay for anything. I was never given that opportunity, which weighed heavily on my victimhood heart. I was called into the office a couple of times and questioned about my husband's intentions toward the commune, since he had been a major part of the very small insiders group in Pune. I, unfortunately, lied and said I was in touch with him all the time and that he fully intended to live here. I was never in touch with him and made it all up for fear that they would think badly of me for not being important enough for my husband to want to be with me, much less call me once in a while. I was deeply intimidated by the ruling mas and was not able to be brave enough to tell the truth. (I'm sure this added significantly to my lack of self-love.) One of them had been married to Tosh before and was particularly interested in his well-being. And the naked truth was he was part of the rebellion on the outside against Ma Anand Sheela. Recently, I was told he greatly regretted his rebelliousness and separation from the ranch and the community. He had been such an integral part of the commune in Pune and cherished those memories. He was in a state of depression until he died. But his funeral was attended by hundreds of sannyasins who knew him and loved him.

About this time, Sheela was in the news for constantly trying to outsmart the state and county officials with many different creative ways to counter their efforts to deny us permanent status as a city. Rather than explain everything in detail here, I'll refer you to Sven Davisson's article "The Rise and Fall of Rajneeshpuram," the current Netflix series called *Wild Wild Country*, and an hour-long video by Oregon Trust in a series called *The Oregon Experience: Rajneeshpuram*. All are excellent representations of the truth as I experienced it.

PING! My first ride of the day began in Mill Valley and ended near the Embarcadero in San Francisco with a woman psychologist of about forty-five. She wanted to know why my name was Yamini, and I told her. This began a twenty-five-minute discussion about my experience in Pune and at the Oregon ranch with Bhagwan, because her mother and father were also sannyasins. Unfortunately, her experience would confirm the darkest of unfounded beliefs

about Rajneesh. She was a young child when her mother and father left for Pune just two months after giving birth to her baby sister, leaving them both to be raised by an aunt and uncle. Her impression was that her parents had been ordered to come to Pune and leave their children behind.

Now she believes that it is a cult and no one is allowed to be themselves or do anything that doesn't correspond to Rajneesh's dictates. She thought that we all worshipped Bhagwan because we had to wear red and a beaded necklace, called a *mala*, with his picture in a locket. I tried to tell her that worshipping him, or anyone for that matter, was completely against his teachings, and that his signature quote was "Don't look at the finger pointing to the moon, look at the moon." And his message to me was "Be a light unto yourself." I told her that he was all about dismantling widely held belief systems so that we could form our own opinions and discover our own authenticity. But she had wounds that were too deep to penetrate and departed still unconvinced. Coincidentally, the next ride I picked up, a block from where I left her, was an Indian couple who knew all about Osho (Bhagwan) and read many of his books and understood and greatly admired his teachings, even though they were not sannyasins.

I will explain only my own personal experience of some of the events that took place and a few retrospective thoughts. To me it all began with one of Sheela's bright ideas: the sudden influx of about three thousand homeless men transported from around the US by over a hundred yellow school buses driven by sannyasins. They were housed in available A-frames and in a tent city erected for them. They were supposedly rehabilitated here from drug and alcohol abuse by certain drugs given them, and when they were strong enough to work, they were given jobs alongside sannyasins. They ate their meals with us, and I noticed many of them would pour a heap of sugar on their potatoes and vegetables. They danced with us at the disco, and it was like watching a hardened criminal become docile and sweet, mingling their energy with ours.

We heard they were here to help us vote in the Dalles (the county seat) to gain power in the local government to secure our rights as an established city. Many of them assimilated with us and became sannyasins. I remember groups of them gathering in front of the mall and breaking into spontaneous rap sessions. It was the first time I ever heard rap music. They would speak a story with a drumbeat, with each person adding a sentence ad infinitum until the group felt the story was completed. Rap sessions could go on for up to forty minutes. Someone would invariably do a Michael Jackson moonwalk to the music. It was a joyous thing to behold, and everyone within hearing distance would be uplifted.

Soon after, news organizations from around the world got hold of the story and came to Rajneeshpuram to see for themselves and report their impressions. All the articles were posted on a board downtown the next day, and we were amazed and saddened to see that almost all of them made up stories that were untrue and cast us in a bad light. It got so ridiculous I even had one reporter follow me into a public bathroom. Luckily, the door had a lock on it.

Coming on the heels of all this publicity, the Guardian Angels took up residence in Antelope and came into the ranch daily, trying to talk some of us out of believing that Bhagwan was legitimate and cautioning us to leave for our own good. In addition, we had a loud Bible-thumper on the main street across from the mall, shouting warnings of hellfire and damnation. It was a circus. Meanwhile, unbeknownst to most of us, the government was surveying us with airplanes and staging a coup. According to Sven Davisson, who investigated the whole thing extensively, we could have ended up just like the Branch Dravidians did many years later. Since our first day at the ranch, we had heard of threats on Bhagwan's life and on the commune almost daily. Locals had stickers on their cars and trucks with Bhagwan's picture and a gun sight across his face. We tried to make friends with them, but they were hostile from the beginning. However, they were not the enemy. They were bit players in a nationwide drama that almost ended in mayhem.

Meanwhile more of Sheela's tactics included taking away some of our rights and small benefits, such as snacks at break times, and making us work longer and harder. She would assert her authority in every workplace, saying how things should be done, even if she didn't know what she was talking about. In my case, she paid a visit to us in the restaurant and instructed us to make guacamole "the correct way" with twelve avocados, one small lemon, one cup of milk, and a dash of salt. I was flabbergasted, but of course, I didn't speak up. This was to position herself as the undisputable head of the commune and make us her slaves. Later we learned she had built a bunker under her house loaded with books on how to enslave a large group of people. Not coincidentally, Bhagwan suddenly came out of his silence and gave talks nightly to a small group of sannyasins, which were videotaped and later played for the rest of us in Buddha Hall. It was learned that on one of the tapes he told everyone not to believe anything Sheela said, because she had evil intentions. That tape was never shown, and Sheela announced that it somehow got lost or destroyed. Some sannyasins knew better, and the word got out.

Another disquieting occurrence was the appearance of four Uzi-armed female sannyasins walking alongside all four corners of Bhagwan's car during his drive-bys. There were also two Ford Broncos with armed sannyasins: one in front and one in back. Sometimes a helicopter whirred overhead with sannyasins pointing Uzis at the crowd. It was surreal. What happened to us? We were peaceful, loving sannyasins now suddenly carrying machine guns! We knew we had a small municipal police force, but we never knew they would be used in such a way. Most of us had nothing at all to do with guns or weapons of any kind. Our weapon of choice was meditation and joyful celebration dancing on the heads of hatred, fear, and self-doubt. I wish the leaders had embraced that form of weapon instead of playing into the fear and the illusion the world believed about us.

My take on all the scandals and Bhagwan's noninvolvement and nonintervention is that it happened precisely as it should, given our spiritual immaturity. We were all wrapped up in our little ego trips, unaware of the bigger picture, allowing everything to happen because we had only the barest understanding of our individual power and connection to Source. Not one of us stood up to Sheela as we watched her abuse her power over us, slowly taking away our rights and pushing us to work harder and longer hours.

To me it looks like a similar thing is going on in our government today, where the truth is being labeled as fake news and lies are rampant and excused for only being "alternative" truths. Also, too many congressmen are afraid to speak truth to power and do what's right, for fear of not being reelected or alienating their donors. Similarly, we were all afraid of being thrown off the ranch. Thus we were like little lemmings giving away our power, willing to believe the lies and kiss-assing our leaders in order to stay with our beloved Bhagwan. I guess I wasn't the only opportunist in existence then.

Disclaimer: Decades later, I have heard many rumors about Bhagwan's sex life from people who weren't there but apparently knew someone who was. They say he had many young lovers and was also a voyeur, purposely setting up sexual trysts with couples so that he could witness their lovemaking. I have to say that those rumors never circulated around the ranch at any time, or at the very least, never reached my ears. I couldn't even imagine such a thing. Maybe I was too far out of the loop or just too deaf, dumb, and blind because of my devotion to Bhagwan to let any of that in. And why should I have? Such lies are a regular phenomenon around people of power by those who fear the unknown and fear their own lack of self-power, self-awareness, and self-love. They feed on rumor and "fake news" that bolster their hateful, misguided opinions.

PING! I pulled up to Amelia, a lovely windblown blond-haired woman standing alone on Union Street in San Francisco, just outside her office. We exchanged greetings, and I noticed she seemed preoccupied and even distraught about something. I waited for her to settle in and then asked, "How's your day going?" hoping to get some response that would open up a more revealing and personal conversation. She didn't disappoint. Right away she went into a lengthy monologue about her last client, whose story had brought up a lot of personal feelings. I sneaked a glance at her expressive suntanned face, which was becoming red with emotion, and her clear blue eyes, welling up noticeably with tears. Apparently, the woman she was talking about had had a childhood similar to hers, and it had touched her deeply, reminding her of her own life experiences.

She took out a Kleenex and wiped away the moisture around her eyes as she continued, in between hiccups. "Excuse me, I seemed to have gotten the hiccups. This sometimes happens when I get (*hic!*) emotional. This poor woman has been to hell and back! I thought I had an exclusive patent on this one (*hic!*) but apparently not. Like me, she was beaten every day by her schizophrenic mother from the time she was just a toddler (*hic!*), unbeknownst to her father. Her mother always told him that the bruises and scars were from household accidents (*hic!*). Once when she was seven, her mother locked her in the basement for two days without food or water while her father was gone on a (*hic!*) business trip."

I interjected, "Wow! That's unbelievable!"

"Yes, and when he came home and found her, he didn't believe her story (*hic!*), knowing she had an overblown imagination that always tended on the (*hic!*) dramatic side. He thought she may have accidentally locked herself in the basement for an hour or two (*hic!*) while her mother went shopping. My story is similar in that my mother was having affairs while Dad was gone on business trips (*hic!*), and she would beat me and threaten to kill me if I ever told him. Once I did tell him, but he (*hic!*) didn't believe me, as mother was very clever in manipulating the truth and convincing him otherwise. While he was out of the house, she hit me so hard I fell to the floor unconscious."

I cried, "Oh no, how awful!"

"He also accused me of making up stories or exaggerating the truth and wouldn't believe anything I said. That's the part that hurt the most. Hmmmm, I think my hiccups are over now, thank God!" She sighed and said, "Gee, I didn't mean to burden you with these gruesome childhood stories. Somehow I felt it was safe, and I needed to talk to someone about it before I exploded! You seemed so open and available." I nodded with my mouth still open from disbelief.

She looked at me and asked if I was OK. I nodded again and tried to smile reassuringly. She seemed to be fully recovered from her emotional breakdown, expressed primarily through the hiccups. I dropped her off at her destination, and she apologized and also thanked me for lending an ear and hoped we would somehow meet again. I felt a strong connection to this remarkable woman. Oddly, right after she left, I got the hiccups.

15

WHAT I DID FOR LOVE
And Love Is All There Is

My overzealous opportunism completely backfired on me. Instead of fitting in with the ruling class on the ranch as the wife of Tosh, I was shunned and excluded and eventually kicked out.

This brings me to the inevitable culmination of my ranch experience, when I was forced to start paying $450 a month to stay. I had no money and my parents had all but disowned me, so I could not and would not ask them for help. Instead, I set about begging fellow sannyasins for money and was able to get the first month's rent. I naively thought this would change their minds and allow me to stay without paying. I was very proud of overcoming my loathing and fear of begging by actually getting results. Apparently, the mas in charge didn't share my self-congratulatory opinion. So they asked for another $450, which I again managed to round up. But when they asked me a third time, I knew it was useless, so I quit and agreed to leave in three days.

I was devastated. I doubled over with uncontrollable spasms of pain as tears poured from my eyes like waterfalls for three days. On the last day, a moment of awakening occurred when I looked up through wet puffy eyes to see Bhagwan on the TV in the hotel bedroom I was cleaning, repeating over and over again, "Be a light unto yourself." *Oh, beloved Bhagwan, you know me so well. How can I leave you?*

But I did. And when I took my seat on the plane back to LA, something amazing happened. It felt like a strange but beautiful entity had completely taken over my body and mind, and I had a feeling of profound serenity and peace. Instead of tears, words of wisdom began pouring from my mouth as I gathered a small group of passengers around me who hung on every word.

I didn't know me. *Who the hell am I?* I asked that question a million times at the workshop in India, but this was a whole different thing. I was suddenly inhabited by a very unfamiliar energy, certainly not the poor, pitiful victim I had been so comfortable being most of my life. That old, worn-out pair of shoes had been replaced with a shiny new pair that would take me on a whole new journey of self-discovery.

I recently watched a video about The Farm, a commune in Tennessee, which began in the sixties and had roughly 1,500 residents at the peak of their existence. They were a group of hippies who gave all their money to the commune with the understanding that they had part ownership (moral, not legal) of the property and that they would be taken care of, as it was their obligation to help take care of others. They were avowed vegetarians and grew their own food and built everything from the ground up, like we did. They were a lot less sophisticated than we were in their building achievements, but they managed to sustain the commune for twenty-five years.

What is so interesting is the juxtaposition of their experience with ours. What eventually brought them down was a complete reversal in philosophy when they ran out of money. They decided people had to start paying dues and therefore go to work on the outside. They began imposing strict rules and deposed their spiritual leader, an ordinary guy who had gained everyone's love and respect with his leadership skills and pure and simple wisdom. He was against the new plan, so they voted him out. The heart and soul of the project was impaled. Soon they started leaving in droves, and the commune came to an end around 1985, exactly the same time Rajneeshpuram ended with the departure and imprisonment of Bhagwan. Our demise began with Ma Anand Sheela's greed for power and the gradual oppression experienced by the members. Another similarity was the fact that The Farm was secretly observed for years by the FBI, who finally raided the commune believing they were cultivating fields of marijuana, which actually turned out to be kale.

I was deeply impacted by this video, remembering our own innocence and pureness of intentions having been corrupted eventually by people of lesser values and questionable intentions. It is a bittersweet memory in this day, where we are now becoming numb to the daily dose of nefarious absurdity and dark rhetoric in our politics and the unfathomable violence occurring here and abroad.

16

I CAN SEE CLEARLY NOW
An Artist and Dabbler in the Supernatural

M y new shoes were broken in on the streets of Whittier, where my mother reluctantly let me stay in her upstairs garage apartment. Dad's wife refused to let me stay with them. I was not exactly welcome at Mom's either, but this actually became the perfect temporary solution in so many ways. Being thrown into this situation with my mother brought us closer together like never before. There was some tension at first, but in time, we found out who we were for each other and developed a kind of mutual respect on a level that hadn't existed before. We went beyond mother and daughter, with all the baggage of our prior history, to becoming good friends. I had a whole new appreciation of her, and she began to understand and appreciate me from a much different perspective. My rampant narcissism had given way to a more caring and mature individual ready to pitch in and help and to take responsibility for her life. It took my mother a while to call me Yamini, but once she did, all connections to our past negative relationship seemed to melt away.

Having totaled my car before going to the ranch, I was left with only my "new shoes" and the local bus line as my modes of transportation for the first two weeks. I was in good shape, having done physical labor nine hours a day seven days a week at the ranch, so I was well prepared. I walked and bused to interviews for jobs and bused to the job where I was hired part-time as a typist and receptionist.

Finally, my dad offered to help buy me a used car. He picked out a Volkswagen Diesel Rabbit, which would have been OK if it didn't have diesel fumes and a noisy engine, and if it wasn't almost as bumpy as the truck I drove on the ranch. Beggars can't be choosers, so I accepted it with gratitude. At least he hadn't completely disowned me, and fatherly love was again possible. This poor excuse of a car actually did the job of getting me from point A to points B and C. Point B was my job and point C was the Utsava Rajneesh center in Laguna Beach, where I meditated, danced, ate lunch, and socialized with my beloved sannyasin friends every Sunday.

PING! **Standing on the corner of Hyde and Beach at Fisherman's Warf were two thirty-something couples wearing Red Sox T-shirts, waving happily at my approach. They were going to the Giants vs. Red Sox game at AT&T Stadium, of course. This was a twenty-nine-minute drive for less than two miles' distance. My GPS was crazy that day. Thinking it knew what it was doing, I followed instructions exactly and wound up going in circles many blocks away from the drop-off location. They didn't seem to mind and began laughing at a private joke about lawn gnomes. Being a little high on beer, they had a hard time pronouncing it, saying something like "Who's got a long nose?" and several variations thereof. The car literally shook with laughter.**

I asked what it was all about, and they elected to let one of the girls explain the "real" urban legend around lawn gnomes. They all said they were from Sacramento, and I began to think maybe this was one of Sacramento's secret attractions. She said that generally if you place a lawn gnome in your front yard, you are advertising that you're a swinger and that the game is on. I wondered out loud how the little old ladies with lawn gnomes in their yard dealt with the constant knocks on their doors for

some custom they knew nothing about. We all howled. I told them I had to put this in my book, and they began negotiating for a penny apiece per book sold. I remarked, "That's even funnier than your lawn gnome story."

After about six weeks and six visits to Laguna, I hooked up with a few other sannyasins that wanted to go in together on renting a big house with four to six bedrooms in Laguna. I drove around one day into the hills of Laguna and happened upon a beautiful modern wood-and-glass house in a cul-de-sac with a For Rent sign. The door was wide open, and no one was on the property but me. This was a good omen, no doubt. I walked into a three-story palace with huge two-story windows overlooking a half-acre of beautiful gardens, a gazebo, three redwood decks (one for each level), and a Jacuzzi. This was our Valhalla on Meadowlark Drive. We took it, and several others joined us for a total of ten residents in six bedrooms. I paid a little more for a room to myself, which was on the bottom floor with French doors out to my own deck.

I set out to find a job in Laguna and landed one with a local chiropractor as his assistant and receptionist. He taught me a lot about alternative healthcare, and I assisted in administering healing procedures as well as managing the front office. Turns out, his wife was also a sannyasin, and her name coincidentally was Yamini. (I am not under any illusion as to why he hired me.) I don't believe in luck, but there was something wonderfully mysterious about our connection. He was a sannyasin "wannabe" who went with us to meditations and parties at Utsava, wearing his obligatory red shirt and a hippie rainbow headband. I thought it a bit silly and strange but kept my opinion to myself, of course.

I began my exploration into the arts and metaphysics and later became an art festival creator/producer. It started with a ceramics class, after which I immediately bought a kiln and set up a studio in the garage. I spent twelve to fourteen hours a day on weekends and five to six hours some weeknights making ceramic jewelry, decorative masks, and crystal light boxes (popular at the time). I experimented with all kinds of shapes and glazes and couldn't wait to see how they turned out after firing. It became an obsession. I soon had enough inventory to start selling and participated in local fairs. What I didn't sell, I kept as gifts or for my own enjoyment

I also participated in a local channeling group every Tuesday and Friday night. About ten of us, including the other Yamini, gathered in South Laguna in a house belonging to a woman named Pam, who channeled Quan Yin and an extraterrestrial called Katar. Once, we all witnessed Katar's flying saucer, which hovered over the ocean very near to us for a good seven minutes. Earlier when he spoke, he had promised to show us his vehicle, and then, while Pam was channeling Quan Yin, it suddenly appeared. Not believing our eyes, we all looked out the window at the scene behind her. She always sat facing us in front of a big bay window overlooking the ocean. There was no denying that this was a spaceship, and there were ten witnesses who could testify to that reality. We never saw it again.

Every night, the sessions usually put us all in a trance, which we later tapped into, and with Pam's help, some of us learned how to channel our own enlightened disembodied entities for each other. In our house there were three of us who had been trained by Pam to channel and did so for each other, usually at night. The sessions always left us blissed out with love and a heightened level of awareness.

One day I went to the library to find art books as inspiration for my ceramic creations. One artist who stood out for me was Alphonse Mucha from the Art Nouveau era. I brought home a book of his work, and that night I inadvertently channeled him with his mixed European accent. I was fully conscious and could enjoy his messages as much as everybody else. He turned out to be very funny and light-hearted but spot on with his answers for some who confirmed that fact. The next day, I opened the book and saw a picture of him, but it was a double exposure, causing him to look like a ghost as he merged with his living room background. I felt this was another demonstration of his humor by alluding to my experience of him the night before. (Recently while Googling him, I found many well-defined photographs and wondered why the author had picked one that was obviously a mistake!)

One of us in Pam's group, a girl named Penny Torres, went on to become a famous channel of Mafu, who has a huge national following and lives and works in Ashland, Oregon, with hundreds of his/her followers. Penny's Mafu is very similar to J. Z. Knight's Ramtha, who appeared on many TV shows and channeled five best-selling books in the eighties. They both inhabit their female channels, making them appear larger and more masculine, and both impart the same messages of "enlightened empowerment." Lately, however, (after three decades) Penny has been publicly denounced by several of her ex-followers as extremely possessive, physically abusive, and an out-of-control drug addict. It has been said that J. Z Knight has also gone off the rails. I'm reminded of the old adage "Absolute power corrupts absolutely." It seems rather odd that an enlightened entity would lead his host toward corruption and abusive behavior, which ultimately raises the question as to their authenticity. But it was all good entertainment for a while, and some valuable teachings were transmitted.

When I knew Penny, there was no hint of a distorted ego. She provides a good lesson for all of us to heed. So many of us are blinded by our own aspirations for greatness or enlightenment and are often led off a cliff by a "shiny new penny" that seduces us into submission. We lose sight of our own inherent greatness by looking outward instead of within.

I always had a tendency to do that myself. Thank God I chose Bhagwan, who wouldn't allow me to become blinded by my attachment to him for very long. Through the confluence of uncanny circumstances and deep meditation, my codependency was curtailed and eventually shattered beyond recognition. He ushered in my new way of being with his intonation of "Be a light unto yourself." His legacy lives on in over two hundred books and has grown substantially relevant in these troubled times.

17

THE AGE OF AQUARIUS
Starfair Visionary Arts Expo Is Birthed

PING! This is not from my Uber app. It's a bell that just went off in my head while driving on a personal trip from Marin to Laguna Beach. I just had a new, provocative thought about my own channeling experience, that who I was actually channeling may have been my past self as Alphonse Mucha.

This may be a little confusing, as I've never heard of anyone channeling a past-life embodiment of themselves, but it could be possible. I had a vision some years ago that I was a lesser-known artist of that era and was kind of a rake (ladies' man), with a mustache just like his, who painted beautiful women and then seduced them only to flippantly dismiss them. This can account for my karma (cause and effect) of being abandoned by so many men I've loved in this lifetime. However, I don't want to besmirch his reputation if, in fact, he wasn't me. But I Googled his biography, and sure enough, he didn't get married until age forty-six and had been well known for his posters of beautiful women since his early twenties. This gave him plenty of time to fool around. How hard would it be to imagine him being sexually aroused by his gorgeous subjects? The famous actress Sarah Bernhardt commissioned him to do her theatrical posters for six years. Coincidentally, I have photographed a few famous actresses and made them into works of art in my book *The Natural Goddess*.

Another interesting tidbit was how he later developed a passion to elevate women and the feminine aspect in a culture overrun by the industrial age and masculine dominance, which has been my passion for the past ten years. Also, he was a portrait artist, like I've been for years, first as a painter, then as a photographer. Also like me, he became more spiritually inclined later in life and shied away from being commercially successful in lieu of painting for the sake of pure art. Another similarity was his singing ability, which awarded him a free high school education.

But alas, after finding so many parallels that bolstered my theory of being Alphonse Mucha in a past life, I also found out he died four months *after* I was born in 1939. Oh well, it was a great story, so I decided to include it anyway. My belief now is that he is either one of my spirit guides, or his (my) spirit could have entered this body after I was four months old, which correlates with my theory that I spoke about earlier regarding my arguments for abortion.

Hmmmm, who can say for sure what is real and what is pure conjecture? But, I could go on and on about our artistic styles and how they resonate, which further supports my supposition. Nevertheless, it all makes for an interesting story. Maybe the point is: What have I learned in this life that makes me more evolved than who I perhaps was as Alphonse Mucha?

During this time of heightened metaphysical activity and interest, I once again had an out-of-body experience which was very brief but notable. I was taking a nap, and just before drifting off, I lifted above my body and passed by a mirror showing no image of me and reached the ceiling, then fell back into my body. What was striking was that it felt perfectly natural and normal.

After two years, I sold most of my ceramic jewelry and decided to go into something entirely different. I created a pet crystal, like a pet rock, which became a point-of-purchase product sold nationwide. It was called the Moonwater crystal, a small crystal perched inside a clear plastic ring box with a little velvet pouch and a booklet explaining its purpose and how to care for it. I made up a mythical history of the Moonwater crystal from ancient times for added interest. It was highlighted as the gift idea of the month in the National Gift Magazine. This fit well into the crystal craze of the eighties. (A TV production company that produced the show *Touched by an Angel* later hijacked the name Moonwater.) I enjoyed a season of success, but soon my short attention span and overactive creative brain drew me into another adventure.

With 1988 being the year of the Harmonic Convergence, I was struck with a brilliant idea to create a New Age art festival alongside the three well-established art festivals in Laguna Beach. There was a building for sale nestled between the Sawdust Festival and The Art Affair across from the Festival of Arts and Pageant of the Masters. I happened to know the owner of the building and talked him into letting me use it for the two festival months of summer. I had never undertaken such a big project, but for some reason I wasn't the least bit afraid of failure. I had a vision and I went for it.

Many of the sannyasins I knew in Laguna jumped on board to help remodel the building. Coming from having created a whole city in Oregon, I guess they thought this would be a piece of cake, which in many respects it was (a big, fluffy pink cake). We had an architect who drew up a thematic plan for the outside face of the building, which included a six-foot-wide scrim around the top of the building with spray-painted night sky and stars, and a crystal-like STARFAIR in giant letters. The dull yellow building would become peachy pink, with five-pointed stars painted like stained glass in our windows.

Not aware of Laguna's right-leaning politics, I had no fear presenting this to the planning commission. Sometimes it pays not to know. I found out later this never would have come to fruition had it not been for one member on the board who hailed this as "whimsical" and convinced the rest of the board to allow it to exist for that summer only. The local newspaper got wind of this and photographed me in front of the original building, looking at plans, and put it on the front page the following week. No one had thought to create another art festival besides the three that had been in existence for several decades.

While the building was being renovated, I put out a call for exhibitors. We ended up with twenty-seven exhibitors of everything from books and crystals to custom-painted T-shirts, painters, sculptors, a chocolatier, an aura photographer, a virtual light-and-sound show in a headset, and an existential experience of sitting inside a completely mirrored space that made a million of you into infinity. We financed our event through booth fees ranging from five hundred to one thousand dollars each. Most of my exhibitors and team members were women, because I felt they deserved the opportunities and exposure this would give them.

We built a stage for our entertainers with a painted crystal rocket to the moon as a backdrop, with the saying "Inner Space —The Last Frontier" also created by our spray-paint artist. The final touches were potted trees inside and outside and silver sparkle dust on the floor. Mother gave me a gift of ten thousand dollars to help cover the cost. Most of our labor was free or dirt cheap, except for the spray-paint artist and the drug-addicted architect. He kept demanding more and more money to support his addiction to ecstasy and nearly broke us. We didn't make money on this. We charged only one-dollar admission, and the $2,500 we made from that still had us in the red.

Our little peachy pink building caused quite a stir, and the large five-pointed stars (pentagrams)* in each window drew the attention of a born-again Christian activist who thumped his Bible outside and warned of damnation if anyone entered our building.

In the past, the pentagram was commonly seen as a symbol for good and for protection against evil. Today, the pentagram— especially an upside-down pentagram—is the most commonly used symbol of Wicca. The pentagram or the pentacle in Wicca stands for fire, water, earth, air, and spirit.

Thankfully, that only increased the curiosity, and the people poured in. We had live musicians or canned music playing constantly, and the best ones we put on a speaker outside to entice customers. We had a modern dance troupe called Dim Sum who cleverly mimicked passersby by walking behind them and exaggerating their movements to Bobby McFerrin's "Don't Worry, Be Happy."

Thinking back, there were so many wonderful people who ended up donating their time and expertise for the completion of this project when we ran out of money. One such person was the lighting technician. I gave him one of my framed watercolor paintings for his birthday, for which he was humbly grateful. Two other people, my entertainment planner and my publicist, did amazing jobs for the little amount I paid them. We ended up on the whole front page of the *L.A. Times'* Sunday Calendar section, with a wonderful review. The best review, however, came from my mother, who showed up with two of her best friends and gave me a smile and a warm hug as a solid endorsement.

On the last night of the festival, after doing the bookwork and cleaning up the whole place by myself, I went home at midnight and let out a primal scream for eight full minutes at the top of my lungs while everyone was asleep. This, after keeping it together for two solid months of twelve-hour days seven days a week, not including months of preparation and haggling with team members, vendors, and exhibitors. Decorum be damned!

In preparing for the second act and the future of Starfair, one of my exhibitors, a bookstore owner, offered to partner with me for the following year. I welcomed her business expertise and connections, and she was a dear friend. We gathered a new team together from her business contacts and started planning for a new location on Canyon Road in Laguna. What happened next was reminiscent of my experience at CBS when several people under me began conspiring to undermine me and get me fired. It seemed I hadn't changed anything.

It started with the team voting to change the name from Starfair Visionary Arts Expo to something benign and forgettable. It didn't seem to matter that I had already succeeded in establishing Starfair as the fourth festival in Laguna Beach. The plans I drew up and designed for the new look were criticized and thrown out. Every idea I offered was countered with their more favorable ones. Finally, my dear friend, the store owner, came to me and asked me to resign in favor of her and her husband taking over, since Starfair had lost money under my leadership and was sure to be more successful under theirs.

What they didn't realize was that they surgically removed the heart of the project and replaced it with a flat, one-dimensional rendition based on perceived profits. It was summarily rejected by the City of Laguna Beach, and Starfair Visionary Arts Expo was archived into the Laguna Beach history book (if such a book exists).

Several months later, my dear friend, the storeowner, asked me out to lunch and apologized for everything over pasta and wine. I accepted her apology, and we've remained friends to this day.

18

SHE WORKS HARD FOR THE MONEY
The Art of Housecleaning

PING! I headed to Tiburon Tavern in midtown Tiburon and picked up a Mexican gentleman who was very congenial and just a little bit too jovial. Turns out he had just gotten the news that his dad in Mexico City had been diagnosed with liver cancer, and he'd had a little too much to drink to drown his sorrows. Almost everything he said was followed with a jolly "hahaha" and a couple of snorts—his style of laughing. He volunteered the information about his father, who, he said, was such a cool guy because he "graciously" told him the news in a very matter-of-fact way. "You would love my dad if you met him (hahaha, snort, snort). You know what we did? We prayed together over the phone. My father is a pastor, but you know what? I've never prayed with him before. This was the very first time (hahaha, snort, snort)!"

Pretty soon he got me laughing along with him, even though it seemed entirely inappropriate. Then he proudly mentioned that his grandfather was a Mason of 33 degrees, which is very high level. And then he said, "Everybody wonders what happened to ME (hahaha, snort, snort)."

I said, "Oh, you shouldn't demean yourself."

He said, "Oh no, I love myself, really. I love myself (hahaha, snort, snort)! You know what? I'm a server. Like Jesus, I serve people and I love my job."

As I drove on the 101, we passed a long line of stalled cars leading to the Richmond Bridge off-ramp, and he blurted out, laughing, "Those guys are losers (hahaha, snort, snort)!" I agreed and made an L sign with my two fingers on my forehead, and he loved it, saying, "Hey, you're a cool gal. I'm going to roll down my window and flip them (hahaha, snort, snort)!"

I said, "Oh, please don't do that!"

"OK, I won't . . . LOSERS!" he yelled through a closed window. We both cracked up. (Hahaha, snort, snort.)

Soon we got close to his destination, and a pretty blond in shorts and a halter-top was walking on the sidewalk. He rolled down his window and was about to . . . when I said, "Oh no, no, no, don't do that!"

He burst out laughing, saying, "I only wanted to rest my arm on the window ledge. You are so funny (hahaha, snort, snort)!" When he opened the door to leave, he turned to me with a high five and said, "Thanks for the ride, *señorita*."

The following year, 1989, I got a job working as a receptionist at an acupuncturist's office for a while. One of her clients, who owned a housecleaning business, decided she wanted to sell it for $150. Seeing an opportunity consistent with my experience at the ranch, I seized upon it immediately. I couldn't believe my luck, since $150 was less than two days' work. After several weeks of work, I bought a new used Toyota Corolla, which worked perfectly as a vehicle for cleaning supplies and equipment. I cleaned two houses a day, which amounted to ten clients and five hundred dollars cash a week. That was the most I had made since my days at CBS and Warner Bros. I named my business The Art of Cleaning. I can hear my teenage self screaming bloody murder: "What, me, a house cleaner? No friggin' way!" My teenager was OK when it was for a higher cause. What she didn't realize was this was part of that higher cause . . . to expand my awareness and know and love myself more fully.

My career as a housecleaner lasted five years. I took pride in leaving each house in beautiful condition and imagined the pleasure it would give the owners when they returned. I joined a couple of network clubs to promote my business. My mother was amazed that I had been transformed from a sloppy, untidy, narcissistic, and irresponsible artist to a professional house cleaner. Always the epitome of a fastidious housewife, she was so pleased she decided to reward me with a down payment on my own condo in 1992. (My mother was independently wealthy, with multiple stocks in AT&T because of my grandfather's position at Bell Telephone in Canada for many years.)

During this time, I took watercolor classes at Saddleback College and began doing watercolor portraits and fine art pieces for community art shows. I've always had a talent for rendering good likenesses, first with pencils and ink, then pastels, then acrylics, and finally watercolor. I used one network club for my cleaning business and the other for portraits. When I was eight years old, I drew a picture of President Eisenhower, and Mrs. Cox, my third-grade teacher, was so excited about it she mailed it to him. This also points to my interest in politics at a young age. Earlier, I wrote a love letter to General MacArthur when he came home from the war and had a ticker tape parade in his honor in Manhattan. I believed my father when he said MacArthur was a hero. At that young age I even believed him when he said *Democrat* was a dirty word. A few years later that belief would be recalibrated.

Working as a housecleaner allowed me to develop an appreciation for other housecleaners and to transcend any judgments I had for lower-income workers.

19

YOU'VE GOT A FRIEND
One Dies, One Is Born, and Two New BFFs

I moved into my new condo in 1992 with my good friend Joy as a housemate. We enjoyed combining our decorating talents and resources to create a beautiful space for both of us. We had many social gatherings there and shared self-improvement activities, such as relationship workshops and our daily practice of Qi Gong. She was an ordained minister and a business coach and a good friend who was always championing my artistic endeavors. At this time, my mother moved into a fancy retirement home in Yorba Linda, and I made sure to visit her every week. She gave me a shoulder to cry on when things weren't going well in my life. She was the mother I had always wanted as a child. I felt her love and genuine concern, and I also saw that she needed the same encouragement, as she was lonely and living an empty existence apart from family and friends. We filled each other's void at that time.

I got a call in 1995 from my mother's retirement home to come quick—she had been found unconscious. I fainted when I saw her in the hospital, knowing this was probably her last day. My brother and I stayed with her in the hospital room while she was unconscious and struggling to breathe. Unfortunately, she died when I was out of the room taking a dinner break, and I was not able to be with her during her glorious moment of transition. I found out later that she had been under the supervision of two different doctors who never consulted each other when prescribing her medications. Combined, they gave her fourteen different drugs for a variety of ills, and as a result, she had a massive stroke. She was eighty-four, and I think she could have lived to 103, like her mother did, if she had wanted to.

I have carried this resentment toward allopathic medicine for a long time, blaming it for both my mother's and father's deaths. I refuse to take any pills other than daily natural supplements prescribed by a naturopath nutritionist and an aspirin when I absolutely need it for acute pain. At seventy-nine, I can attest to my comparatively youthful appearance and good health due to my daily workouts and my nutritional support and discipline. I'm a "foodie," so it takes a lot of discipline to avoid sugar, wheat gluten, and dairy products—and the truth is, I am a dunce when it comes to sugar.

As for our inheritance, mother was very generous, giving us trust funds that would provide basic living expenses for each of us for a long time. I also received some cash, part of which I invested in stocks. Unfortunately, a year later the stocks took a dive, and I panicked and took my money out.

I could have been a millionaire now if I had let it alone. This is one of my major flaws: my indifference to money; my impatience, or need for instant gratification; and the inability to see the big picture, particularly where money is concerned. I was once accused of being a failure with money because I was a "trust fund baby" and too complacent to give money the respect it deserves. It's pretty well known that most successful people are driven from childhood deprivation. The only deprivation I had was a lack of outward parental displays of affection.

Joy started having a relationship with a sweet, sensitive man in our Qi Gong group who stayed overnight many times. He was desperately in love with her and was not afraid to show it. She did not share his exuberance but liked him enough to let him hang out with her occasionally. He asked her to marry him twice but, given his inability to have a steady income, was met with a stern "no" both times. Then one day she became pregnant, and he thought that now, for sure, she would capitulate. She considered it and then realized his lack of responsibility in life would make him dependent on her. However, she did want to have him in their child's life as the father. He was heartbroken and cried openly at our next Qi Gong class when she announced her pregnancy.

Nine months later, a brand-new love of my life came on the scene one night at a birthing center in Pomona. At midnight, Joy's boyfriend and I drove her, followed by a caravan of her closest friends, to Pomona. At 3 a.m. we were honored to witness the birth of her son, Michael, in a birthing pool of warm water with his father supporting Joy from behind in a seated position as she pulled the child from her body into full view of all of us. She had set up the room with candles and crystals and soft music for his delivery. He was then blessed by each one of us and beautifully by a friend who sang an Irish lullaby. It was a truly sacred moment that none of us are likely to ever forget. Her son, my godson, is now twenty-five and owns his own house in Tacoma, Washington, living with the love of his life. He is a wonderful testament to Joy's devotion and skill in raising him. I was blessed to have been a secondary mother for the first four-and-a-half years of his life.

One night, I attended a Spiritual Singles party on the beach, which formed a circle around a lighted candelabrum, where we sat and discussed social issues. There I connected energetically with a guy I'll call Handy and was flattered by his flirtations, which later drew me into an intimate relationship. He was a big, sandy-haired, husky guy, gentle and sweet and very bright. It had been a while since I'd been with anyone, so I was grateful for the attention. Initially, we had a quietly passionate love affair that lasted about a year. Later, I let it lapse into a platonic relationship. I began faking orgasms with him just to keep him around (until the love of my life showed up). However, he was a great support system for my work, being a natural organizer and talented handyman. We also had a lot of common interests, particularly in spirituality, which he was becoming fully engaged in. It was fun hanging out with him in his world and reaping the benefits of being a couple wherever we went.

PING! I was on my way to my favorite place for chai, the café at Good Earth, when I got a call to pick up someone nearby in Mill Valley. A young couple came running down the hill to the house I was in front of, and they said they gave that address because Ubers can never find her actual address. They looked vaguely familiar. She said she was in the throes of moving in with him in Petaluma, and they were both exhausted and taking a break. I congratulated them and asked where they were going now, and they said The Cantina in Mill Valley. I said, "Oh, I know that place. I had a great experience there once that I'm putting in my book about Uber driving."

There was a brief pause, and then he said, "We know someone who's writing a book about Uber driving . . . wait. . . is your book called *The Joy of Uber Driving*?"

I answered, "Yes . . . oh no, are you Steven with the wire guitar art piece?"

They both shouted, "Yes! That was our second date when you picked us up, and we haven't been back there since. What a coincidence that you are our Uber driver again today!"

I said, "There are no accidents. You guys are very special to me, and now it's two months later, and you're moving in together! How great is that? This will be a follow-up piece in my book, but not if I don't get a hug from you like the last time!" I winked. They didn't disappoint. It was another wonderful day Uber driving.

Before Handy, it seemed like the whole world was populated by couples, and I was the only exception. So, when we walked down the street or into a grocery store or to a party or a movie holding hands,

I felt like I had finally joined the human race. It was no wonder that a year later, he broke off our relationship. Faking it with a sensitive soul such as his was doomed to failure. In retrospect, I was not ready to take responsibility for a real relationship then, but had I been, he might have been the perfect lifelong mate for me. As fate would have it, he found his lifelong mate a few years later.

I needed to learn not to take relationships for granted. They are precious and deserve to be managed with great care and creativity. I also needed to discern between a true hero of a man and a matinee idol type, which I was waiting for as the so-called love of my life.

20

I'VE GOT TO USE MY IMAGINATION
Musical Pillows and LED Shoes

I was still cleaning houses and doing watercolor portraits, but my creative nature sought other outlets. One time, while standing in line at a police station to pay a traffic ticket, I noticed that a beam of light shining through the trees landed on someone's shoes. That gave me the idea for LED lights on sneakers. I excitedly made a prototype and applied for a patent pending and then presented it to Adidas. They turned it down, saying they had their own designers and didn't need any outside ideas. Sure enough, a year later, my idea was copied and manufactured and is still a popular item in kids shoes to this day. I could have handled this a lot better with some expert business and legal help and perhaps the likes of a *Shark Tank* TV program at the time. Oh well . . . I count my blessings, as my creative juices are forever flowing.

Just a few years before anyone, including me, knew anything about smartphones (which were invented in 1992), my next brainchild was my audio pillow, which was a tubular U-shaped pillow in many styles. I used different fabrics including a soft fleece or polyester satin one for the bedroom to a sporty canvas one for the beach with a shoulder strap and pockets for keys, change, and so on. It doubled as both an audio headset and a neck pillow, with the ends placing the microphones at ear level. I rented a power sewing machine and bought yards and yards of different fabrics and fillings and findings. I researched the best earphones and small radio components and spent countless hours on the machine making my samples. I visited several local factories and got estimates. Even though there were other audio pillows in existence, I received a utilities patent for this model. However, I could not get funding for the manufacturing and distribution of this product after two years of product design and development and promoting unsuccessfully to potential financial backers. Once again, I missed grasping the brass ring, but I chalked this one up as a creatively fulfilling experience. It would have become obsolete with the onset of the smartphone in a few years anyway.

Handy was instrumental in two of my biggest career undertakings: he introduced me to the world of computers, helped me select one, and taught me what I needed to know about it. And he sold me his Canon EOS Elan camera and all his studio equipment as partial payment for a ten-thousand-dollar loan I gave him from my inheritance. He had been an unemployed engineer for two years. He was extremely diligent and responsible in paying off the loan, which tells you what a true and valuable friend he was/is. Others, who had heard of my inheritance and immediately pounced on me for badly needed funds, were not so true and honest. One still owes me twenty thousand dollars. She left town for parts unknown and hasn't been heard from since. The other, who owed me five thousand dollars, kept coming up with excuses until I just gave up. I am not the litigious kind. Their problems were a lot worse than mine. It's not my job to seek justice or self-righteous validation at their expense. The universe will deliver whatever justice or lessons they need to learn.

Sometimes I fail to listen to my gut and discern what's right or true and how to say "no" to what isn't. Perhaps more importantly, I didn't have enough self-esteem to simply demand or negotiate a payment plan, which would have given me a clearer path to self-love as well. Handy initiated his own payment plan and stuck to it.

Before selling my condo, I moved back to Laguna Beach into a duplex apartment that I lived in for the following eighteen years. Joy and her son remained in the condo until it was sold. I kept up my commitment to Michael as a devoted godmother for two more years, taking him places he loved, such as Burger King, indoor play centers, a park, or the beach, two or three days a week. At age four and a half he had long blond hair and became a supermodel for some of my favorite black-and-white photos. Being around Michael kept me feeling young at heart while playing an important role in his growth.

PING! It was dark and a thirteen-year-old boy named Jared emerged from the bushes surrounding Scottsdale Pond (a small park in Novato) to signal he was the rider that called. A sweet young man with Pokémon* pins on his cap entered my car, shivering from the cold and partly from fear. He had been alone searching for another Pokémon when a group of three rowdies started following and taunting him, threatening to steal his cap. He said that he'd pretended to call the police when he was really calling Uber. He said this kind of thing happens to him a lot, and he doesn't understand why. I perceived it was because he was so sweet and innocent. But he also said that he felt protected by unseen forces. While he was calling Uber, he said a police car with flashing lights sped by and the gang freaked out and ran the other way. He hid in the bushes while he was waiting for Uber, just in case they returned. I was impressed with the young man's composure. He elicited a strong desire for me to protect and mother him but strangely, at the same time, respect him for the adult he was becoming.

*Pokémon GO is a popular game app on smartphones that has players go out of their homes to hunt for and collect virtual creatures in augmented reality.

21

DREAM WEAVER
Humanimal Rises from the Ashes

I was excited to be back in Laguna, having found a beautiful, large two-bedroom duplex apartment with a whitewater ocean view. I laid down a new carpet and bought bedroom and living room furniture from various antique and secondhand furniture stores in the area, which I refurbished myself. Being two blocks from the beach and a twenty-five-minute walk to downtown Laguna, I was in heaven!

My affair with Handy was over after little more than a year, but our friendship was strong, and he was always available to give me whatever assistance I needed in my new digs. He used his abilities as a handyman and organizer to help pay off the loan. According to the plan, it wouldn't be paid off for another four or five years, with interest. He was particularly helpful in building my darkroom from a room formerly used as a laundry room. There was a large extra room with an outdoor entrance on the side of the building that we converted into my photo studio.

I studied photography privately from two of Laguna's best, Robert Hansen and Bill Agee. Digital photography had not come into existence yet, so the darkroom was a major part of the creative process. I fell in love with this process the same as I had done years ago with clay slab work and the ceramic kiln, by spending hours upon hours

in the darkroom perfecting my black-and-white images. I was fascinated with the works of Jerry Uelsmann, who superimposed multiple
images, creating surreal landscapes. His images were used for the
opening credits of the TV series *X-Files*. I also dabbled in infrared
photography, which made leaves on trees white and glowing against
black skies. Many years of art photography and professional portrait
photography were born at this location with the help and support of
my friend Handy.

One day, before moving to Laguna, I witnessed smoke billow-
ing on the other side of the hills that separated Laguna Hills from
Laguna Beach. Turning on the TV, I saw what turned out to be the
great Laguna fire of 1994, which destroyed over three hundred homes.
Later, my morbidly creative mind seized on the prospect of using
burned-out homes as artistic backdrops for nude portraits.

I picked for my model Wave, a strikingly handsome guy who was
the host at a popular Laguna restaurant. I knew him also from a spiritual workshop he'd facilitated earlier that year. He had beautiful eyes,
a full head of wavy shoulder-length hair, a square jaw and straight
nose, and a perfect, lithe and lean body. I took nude photos of him
huddled in burned-out fireplaces or roaming the crumbled remains
of a burned-out house or a barren, ash-filled treescape. In my photos
he looked androgynous, and in some photos he looked more like a
woman than a man. I called him my "Humanimal." Together, we made
up a story of a humanlike creature born in the sand dunes of Death
Valley, as a grown man roaming the world and seeing the destruction
of nature by modern man. Deciding to take a trip to Death Valley to
explore photographic possibilities, we found an army museum in the
desert with World War II tanks. I had him straddling one of them in
the nude to show the juxtaposition of a beautiful natural man and a
death machine. Death Valley itself did not give me what I wanted for
his birth picture.

I was developing a crush on this godlike creature, but unfortunately, he did not have the same feelings for me. I think he was not as connected to his animal side as he was to his spiritual side. Unknowingly to me then, he was a gift in a deeply spiritual way. He had a childlike quality that was very disarming and innocent. Oftentimes, he helped me to key into a bigger picture of what was essential and important as opposed to what was expedient or commercially viable. Meanwhile, I signed up for a photographic trip to the Grand Canyon with my teacher Bob Hansen. I took Wave with me, and we shared a room with a single bed to save money. This was awkward to say the least, since I was hot and he was not.

On the way to the Grand Canyon, we stopped at Fire Canyon near Las Vegas and created some more incredible images. One of my favorite shots was with him buried in the red sand, showing the outline of his stretched-out body from a low angle that elongated his legs. This could easily be his birth shot. Another shot was in the crevice of a cliff and another lying on a boulder like a lizard. He was so easy to photograph because he was completely in tune with my vision. The Grand Canyon itself was not amenable to the kind of shots I was looking for, so we left Hansen's class and went on our own. We encountered a controlled forest fire nearby. I told him to strip down and run through the smoke-filled forest. This elicited one of my best images. At one point we had to hunker down, hearing the clopping of hoofs from two mounted police passing by on the street near us.

Back home in my studio, I took several shots of him against a white background. At the time, he was babysitting a white python snake, which we brought to the studio in my car. This was a rather freaky experience, as Wave was holding him in the back seat and decided to let him loose enough to slither between the two front seats to greet me. "Geez Louise!" and other less ladylike expletives came out of my mouth. He laughed, but it was all worth it, as we got some very interesting shots. I now had a portfolio of stunning and unique black-and-white nude portraits, which I spent hours perfecting in my darkroom. A local bookstore allowed me to set up a showing with seventeen of these enlarged, matted, glass-framed images. I wanted to create a book of these with the title and a fable called *Humanimal*, but he had other ideas that conflicted with mine, so my book idea was laid to rest. Perhaps in the future I'll give it another go.

Later, I went on another class photo adventure in downtown LA, escorted by our own private police officer. We went to the underbelly of LA, where I got some of my most prized black-and-white shots, which I later hand painted and used in many of my superimposed images with Humanimal.

PING! **Once in a while someone comes into your life that inadvertently influences you in a profound way. Just such a person entered my car and gave me a smile that lit up the whole interior as though a floodlight had been turned on. He was bubbling over with joy, and I had to ask what happened that made him so happy. Graciously and unexpectedly, he crooned, "I just got picked up by a beautiful woman Uber driver!"**

I looked askance at him and said, "You know, I'd take you wherever you wanted to go just as fast if you hadn't said that. But thank you anyway."

He flashed his brilliant smile and countered, "I meant it, really!" He sat back and put on his ear plugs connected to his iPhone and started humming while I concentrated on my GPS directions and drove to his destination. I noticed he was scribbling something while humming and then words came tumbling out in rhyme as a song was being born. I knew better than to interrupt his creative flow, but I was really curious who this guy was.

There was something about him that screamed VIP! He was tall and big and had a look that could be defined as happy and at peace with himself, belying years of grief and sadness. I wanted to know more about him, but there was no time left to

start a conversation as we approached his destination. Instead he seemed to read my mind and handed me a card announcing an event coming up next month in Marin called Soul Song, with his name, Gary Malkin, as the producer/creator and seven-time Emmy award-winning composer. He then reached into his brief-case and pulled out a CD, which he gave me as a gift. This was the best tip ever! I was grateful for having connected with such a beautiful spirit while Uber driving. The following month, I went to the event and was part of an audience of about two hundred people singing and dancing to rapturous music sometimes sung and played on the piano by Mr. Malkin. After the event, I stood in line to congratulate him. He remembered me and gave me a big bear hug.

In 1996 I was juried into the Festival of Arts with my custom box-framed images of Humanimal, one with him superimposed on railroad tracks in a fetal position, a shot of him as a giant looming over a street of abandoned buildings, and one of his screaming face superimposed within graffiti. All images were hand painted in a sur-real way.

I designed and made my booth to look like moldy cracked con-crete walls with moss creeping over them, in keeping with my photo-graphic theme. Humanimal and his friend helped me build the booth. I successfully sold many of my pieces and was asked to demonstrate how I'd hand painted my black-and-white images in the demo booth four or five times during the summer show.

With a very high score, I learned, I was juried back in for the fol-lowing year and had a whole different exhibit with photo sculptures. I created environments out of concrete, within which the photo merged into the space. But this time, I had employed a couple of female nudes as well as Wave. I carelessly forgot to get a release from one of the models, and she sued me for twenty thousand dollars for "defaming her." Turns out, she was a regular mud wrestler at a local OC bar, and my lawyers brought it down to two thousand dollars as a frivolous lawsuit. I couldn't believe her disingenuousness, when the images I had of her were beautiful works of art, while she was a sex performer in a bar. I tried to emotionally detach myself, but there were larger consequences: when the word reached the head of the jury committee, I was subsequently juried out for the following year. A couple of the jurors were surprised, because they had given me high scores. However, they said the head of the art festival had made them use pencils that year instead of pens when marking their ballots. Politics was a common occurrence even at the Festival of Arts. Any unresolved anger I had by then was fully expressed as I smashed many of the beautiful pieces I had made with her image and threw them in the trash. Anger does not justify such a stupidly destructive act. . . . I regret it now.

After the 1997 festival debacle, I decided to focus on building a career doing children and family portraits in Laguna. Once again, Handy to the rescue as he helped black out my wall of sliding-glass doors to the patio and convert my living room into a photo studio. My career blossomed and included family portraits on the beach, which was very popular and sought-after. I set up a photo tent at school festivals in Laguna and once at the annual Sawdust Christmas Festival, which increased my customer base each time.

The following years, my business grew as I advertised in schools and at network clubs and created a niche with black-and-white vintage photos of children. I scoured eBay for vintage children's clothes, furniture, and props and developed a large wardrobe for both boys and girls. About this time, my beloved cat Hercules wandered into my life through the back door and decided to stay. He became a prop in one of my favorite portraits of a young girl in a vintage dress sitting on a child's wicker couch with him. He was a magnificent ginger-and-white long-haired Maine Coon cat with almond-shaped eyes. I got very attached to this furry being of unconditional love. He was

King of the Hood. Everyone on the street knew him and loved him. He brought me gifts of live birds, mice, or lizards every day, which I learned how to capture and then relocate. He was my best friend. When I held him, he would look up at me lovingly and purr and then snuggle under my armpit.

22
WIND BENEATH MY WINGS
A Joyful Unexpected Reunion

Twenty years ago, I remember receiving a phone call one Thursday night from a woman who asked, "Do you remember giving birth to a baby girl thirty-two years ago?"

My heart leaped out of my throat. I couldn't breathe. . . . "Are you, are you . . . ?"

"Yes, my name is Molly, and I've been looking for you since I was thirteen." I flew to Oakland the next day and spent the weekend with her and her husband in Concord. When we met, we both couldn't stay standing. We stumbled to the nearest bench, sat, held each other's hands, hugged, and looked deeply into each other's eyes for the longest time. The first thing she told me was that she was so grateful that I gave her life and gave her up to such a wonderful family. She knew all about me. She had a whole dossier on me compiled by her tech-savvy brother. We both had applied to the same central agency for birth parents and children to find each other.

When we got to her place, Molly sat me down in front of the TV and inserted a VHS tape she had compiled of movie clips taken every Christmas of her growing up from age four months to ten years. I got to see how much her family loved her and what a great little entertainer she was, dancing and singing as soon as she could walk. That

Sunday, we went to the Trinity Episcopal Church in San Francisco, where she was a member of the choir of eight professional singers, and she brought me up to the front and introduced me to the congregation. I felt the presence of angels surrounding us.

Later, she and I embarked on a search for Eric, her birth father, the set designer who had nearly fainted in front of my dad and who later worked for Francis Ford Coppola. Turns out, he disappeared off the face of the earth around 1989, but a friend was found who knew where he was. We found Eric in a convalescent home in Burbank, being treated for manic depression. I contacted him, picked him up, and took him to lunch. He was a shell of the man I used to know, but he had a daughter who looked a lot like Molly. He had married the love of his life from college. They were now divorced. I arranged for a reunion with him and his daughter and Molly. When the girls met, they became fast friends, and Molly always arranged to meet her when she came to visit me in Southern California. He died shortly thereafter. She was also able to meet my father in an assisted living home a few months before he died. That was a momentous occasion, as my father suffered from dementia but came out of it miraculously and was completely lucid upon meeting his only granddaughter. (Side note: Before my father died, he was kicked out of that particular assisted living facility for streaking down the hall naked. He was true to his nature right up to the end.)

Unfortunately, my mother had died a year earlier and was never able to meet Molly. I feel sure that she would have adored her and wished perhaps that I had been a bit more like her instead of the wild, unpredictable, immature, self-centered person I had been for her. Mother loved opera and often took me to her favorites, such as *Madame Butterfly*, *La Traviata*, and *La Boheme*, where she would always, on cue, weep at the most lyrical moments. Molly had a well-trained operatic voice, and when she played Katharine in *Kiss Me Kate*, she would have made my mother weep with pride. I must admit, however, that even though mother had difficulty understanding me, she was proud of all my accomplishments and was always there rooting for me in her quiet, unassuming way.

When I returned, I planned a "Hello, Molly" party in Laguna in her honor. About eighty of my closest friends came to celebrate our reunion. The most memorable moment for me is when she sang "Wind Beneath My Wings" to me. There was not a dry eye in the room, including my own.

I did at least two trips a year to San Jose to watch her perform on stage, starring in one of many popular musicals, such as *High Society*, *West Side Story*, *Les Miserables*, and *Kiss Me Kate*. She was usually cast as a strong, contentious woman, like the bitchy mother in *Hairspray* or Mama Rose in *Gypsy*. She won the Lucy Award for her starring role in *The Will Rogers Follies*. I cry every time I hear her in one of her productions. I think it's partly because I lost my own singing voice years ago from years of intense Buddhist chanting. I try to justify it as my sacrifice for spiritual growth.

For Molly, the stage is the perfect backdrop for her social life and a place to grow and sharpen her skills in order to be recognized and appreciated as the talented diva she is. It is also an outlet, where she can express emotions on a grand scale that I think she holds back in real life. (By nature she is very controlled and pragmatic.) This was powerfully clear to me in her final scene as Mama Rose, which brought out such authentic raw emotion that I couldn't help but weep uncontrollably myself. I have never actually seen my daughter get angry or cry, except on stage.

To be fair, there is much of her life I haven't been close enough to share, such as when her first husband left her for a younger woman or when she had breast cancer. She told me how devastated she was when her husband left her. She went on a crying jag for weeks. I was shocked to learn she had breast cancer (which was cured). She never told me about the breakup or the cancer until after the fact.

She still had her adoptive mom and siblings and close friends to talk to, which may have been all the emotional support she needed at that time.

After seeing her in *Gypsy*, I almost became a real-life stage Mama Rose in my desire to see her expand her career to professional status. She informed me she is completely fine being out of the union loop so she can have juicier roles. The life she has now is her dream, not mine. Let me, with my overbearing inner Rose, not interfere. She has made it clear that her real mother is the one who raised her, but she holds a special place in her heart for me and is grateful that I am in her life now.

PING! I have the good fortune to be hired to pick up Julia, an adorable young lady of ten, at her gymnastics school every Monday evening. Her mom, a beautiful French woman, one of the most naturally happy women I've ever met, hired me to make sure her daughter would be safely brought home by a female Uber driver. Tonight was my second time with Julia, who had recently put a subtle streak of blue in her hair for a friend's birthday party.

I don't remember how it started, but she confessed that she didn't believe in the tooth fairy or Santa Claus and asked me if I did. I shook my head and said, "Good Lord, no! Just think about it. In one night a funny fat man rides the sky in a sleigh and drops off presents for four billion kids worldwide." She agreed that it was "totally illogical." I said, "Right, but I believe in magic and that everyone has some kind of magic powers." I pointed to the sky and said, "There, I just moved a cloud."

She giggled and said, "Oh, I'm not stupid." Then she dared me to move a restaurant sign she pointed to.

As we passed it on the freeway, I exclaimed, winking, "Look, it moved right past us." She slapped her knee and giggled again, saying that didn't count. "Well, you know, Santa might be an alien with superpowers."

She shouted, "No way, do you know what he looks like? Nothing like an alien!"

I calmly pointed out, "Anything's possible . . . and he could be a shape-shifter."

Right away, she responded with "What a kawinkidink [her word for coincidence]!" She told me that all the fourth graders in her school are now studying aliens from outer space. She informed me that they have great powers, including shape shifting. She also told me today's daily quote: "When you get a lemon, make lemonade."

As we got close to her home, she asked if I liked being in cars. I said, "Of course. Don't you?" She said that it all depends on who's in the car with you and that she liked being in a car with me. Well, I just melted into a warm pile of goo!

I often wonder if I would have made a good mother. I do have a propensity to want to guide and influence people to become the best they can be. Did I miss out on an important part of my growth by not embracing the responsibilities of motherhood? I have often transferred that question in my mind to Molly, who I feel would have benefited tremendously in her personal growth if she had chosen to be a mother. But again, who am I to question her choices and decide what would be good for her? Even if I had chosen to keep her and take on the responsibility of motherhood, I still would not have the right to decide her life for her. Khalil Gibran in *The Prophet* says: *"Your children are not your children. They are the sons and daughters of life's longing for itself. They come through you, but not from you. And though they are with you yet they belong not to you."*

She came to visit me in Laguna a few times a year, always staying at a hotel near Disneyland. She had a penchant for Disneyland, which marks one of the most striking differences between us. She would do every ride possible at least three times during a weekend, and she cried real tears when Small World was closed down for renovation. This, from a grown woman of thirty-five! I remember looking at her aghast! I, on the other hand, feel great antipathy toward Disneyland because of its sugarcoated phoniness and how it supplies children with commercial papier-mâché creations instead of inspiring them to use their own creative imaginations. I spent my youth making my own toys, such as paper dolls and miniature landscapes in shoeboxes. I even designed a life-sized wooden car for kids (on paper) and a curved, tubular water slide into the pool (on paper) before it was invented at Water World. Unlike everyone else I knew, I was not excited about the opening of Disneyland.

I agreed to go with her and her first husband to Disneyland twice, to try and understand why she was so devoted to the Disney fantasy. It still eluded me. But I found it somehow endearing and felt vindicated knowing that she must have had a wonderful childhood with her adoptive family and was reliving the youthful experiences she'd had with them at Disneyland. I have since softened my stance a bit, seeing the positive in all the colorful, creative beauty and the sweet, joyous atmosphere that gives parents a place to enjoy with their children.

Two years ago, she sent me another compilation video of her growing up with her family in the suburbs. I noticed she had none of the fancy trappings of an upper-middle-class family that I grew up with. She lived in a mid-sized tract home. But the most remarkable part of all the videos was the demonstrably happy and caring environment her family provided for her. She was the object of all their attention and affection throughout her childhood.

I don't remember ever experiencing such a cohesive and loving family atmosphere. There was very little hugging or kissing or even handholding in our family. My earliest memory is of my mother bottle-feeding me with a surgical mask on her face as per the instructions of her new doctor husband, my father. I also had to wear mittens as a baby to prevent me from sucking my thumb. Hence, I sucked my thumb up through my preteen years. I remember once, while mother was helping me with my piano lessons, I turned to hug her and she pushed me away, saying she didn't want me to become like my Aunt Martha, whom she judged as being "too mushy." My mother knew how to express love only in ways I wouldn't appreciate until I was older: things like redecorating my bedroom; cooking delicious meals; taking me shopping for new clothes; and, when I was in high school, making special and unusual sandwiches for my lunch (like cream cheese and raisins). She was not predisposed to hug or kiss Dad or me spontaneously.

So when I saw Molly's videos, I was both amazed and a little envious. Also, it became clear to me why my overly expressive father sought other means of expressing his love. He was of French heritage and my mom was of a strict British heritage: two vastly different cultures and temperaments.

23

SEND IN THE CLOWNS
Compliments of Match.com

During this time, I was still looking for my matinee idol through Match.com and other Internet dating services. I had started doing this, years before, with little success, as most people lied about their age and looked vastly different in person. They were all "over-the-hill" matinee idols. I looked younger because of my good genes, not because of any pre-dated photos. I would have been far more interested in them had they presented themselves honestly to begin with. I don't mind over-the-hill matinee idols if they're truthful and are comfortable in the skin they now inhabit. But this was only one reason Internet dating didn't work for me. The other was lack of familiarity or history with a person, which put the burden on chemistry and looks after there was some basic agreement on beliefs and personal values. But maybe this is true in any mating situation. It just seems that more emphasis is put on looks with Internet dating.

I will mention only three of my most impactful Internet dating experiences, of which there were many. One time I hit the jackpot with a guy named Nick on chemistry and looks. We seemed to mesh on most of our values and beliefs as well. We spent weeks on the phone before meeting. He was a sexy, good-looking, and generally cheerful traveling salesman and had some business in Orange County.

When we met, we literally started rolling on the floor of my studio in a passionate embrace. We were in steady communication throughout his travels and hitting all the right notes with each other. We were just at the point of commitment when he called from Florida to say that he had also been seeing someone he liked as much as me (which he had forgotten to mention before), but she lived near him in his home state of Florida, so therefore, he was going to go with her.

Crash! Burn! There went another chink in my frayed and threadbare armor. I had been feeling pretty good about myself prior to meeting him, because I'd lost forty pounds on an extreme makeover program. Now, all that self-confidence I had gained was compromised once again. This was another problem I often encountered with Internet dating: the field is wide open and abundant with possibilities. If the slightest flaw or unresolved issue comes into play, or there's someone else younger or prettier than you, it's over before it has a chance to grow into anything meaningful. It seems a bright spotlight is focused on the flaws the moment they show their face.

PING! **I pulled up to an apartment complex and saw a gal and a guy waiting for me. They hugged, and she got into the car and waved goodbye. He looked longingly at her. She smiled. Her name was Tanya, and she was exceedingly beautiful, with long blond hair and clear blue eyes, wearing stylish tattered jeans. She said she was from Serbia and was going back in two weeks, leaving her boyfriend here and going to the one waiting for her in Serbia. She was not attached. I asked, "What are you doing here, and how does the US compare to Serbia?"**

She said she had been on a summer ecology course here, and as far as the comparison goes, there was absolutely none! For starters, the minimum wage there is eighty cents per hour. She said clothes and cars and most merchandise cost the same as here, but all education, including higher education and health care, was free. House and apartment rentals were substantially lower, but

still most people could barely make it each month. However, there was no homelessness problem whatsoever, as everyone took care of their own. (I'm guessing people bunched up in groups of four to eight for their housing.) I asked about the war and lingering conflicts, and she said the Serbs and the Albanians were constantly fighting, and she got caught in the crossfire once. She was shot in the back, but it was from such a distance that it wasn't critical. She was studying ecology and the global warming effect. She planned to move to the US someday but had no immediate plans. She borrowed money to come here and had been working at a bicycle shop to earn enough to pay it back.

I asked about her social life, and she replied that she's young yet and wants to experience as much of life as she can before committing to marriage. She also admitted to me that she made a lot of bad choices when she first came here, going to parties and getting drunk almost every night with wealthy IT guys in San Francisco. She was embarrassed to confess her "crimes" but said I would be the only person who would ever know. Neither her mother nor any of her friends back home would know this part of her life. What her other so-called crimes were have to be left to our imaginations, as she was not willing to be that open even with a stranger. (To respect her privacy, I changed her name.)

Next? Enter Bob and his bubble machine. We seemed to have a good rapport over the phone, so he made a trip down from Sacramento to Laguna and met me at the gazebo overlooking Main Beach. He brought a bouquet of roses, a bubble machine, and a boom box with the song "You Are So Beautiful to Me." He directed me to go to the rocks on the beach below the gazebo, whereupon he turned on his boom box and bubble machine as he kissed me, to the delight of tourist onlookers above. This raised my level of self-esteem considerably and knocked down any red flags I may have had about him . . . for about a week. We both went headlong into marriage plans immediately and spent the week dreaming up the perfect wedding on my front porch. His contribution: red clown noses and an engagement ring that looked more like his high school class ring. We were both in our sixties. As the week wore on with our sexual explorations and adjustments, on the fourth night he made his first big mistake: shaking a little, and with a small voice, he asked if I would agree to have a facelift if he paid for it. It was like a bucket of ice water had been poured all over me. I should have kicked him out then, but I let him hang around three more days as I did my Christmas Festival gig at the Sawdust that weekend.

The following Monday I was in my office, working on the computer to manage all the new business contacts I had acquired, while he lay on my bed watching TV. I was so engrossed I didn't notice a couple of hours later that he had left. Suddenly, my phone rang, and it was my "fiancé" calling while on the road to Sacramento to say it just wasn't working out as he had planned. He was upset because he wanted me to watch TV with him instead of doing my own "business thing." I tried to talk him back, but his mind was made up. Whew! That was a close call! Can you imagine my going through life with a red clown nose, attached at the hip to another clown nose? Even so, there was another chink in my armor.

Next? Along came Dr. Bones. He was an orthopedic surgeon from Arcata, California. We talked for hours on the phone for two weeks before we met. He had gray hair pulled back in a ponytail, which I've always had a thing for. His pictures were not that exciting, but our minds and our spirit were so in sync I fell for him right away. He would riff on a subject with such humor and originality that I was mesmerized. This, I thought, is what I have been looking for all my life. I've always been attracted to off-the-wall brilliant humor, and he had it! We decided to meet in Berkeley where his daughter lived, and he would pay for my hotel room. When we met eye-to-eye at the airport lobby, he was leaning against a column and looked like a

GQ ad, much more handsome in person than his photos revealed. I was immediately caught off guard, and all my walls went up to hide my sudden lack of self-esteem. If he had smiled, it might have been different. But it seems I did not meet his expectations, as he greeted me with a somewhat cool demeanor while he politely handed me a bouquet of yellow roses and a Zen book of poems.

The whole weekend with him was torture as I tried to make him laugh or smile or respond like he cared for me just a little, only to be met with blank indifference. The more I groveled, the more he withdrew. It was obvious I was not in my power. Somehow, I had abdicated my personal power with the belief that I was not enough. It didn't help that the glaring fluorescent light in the hotel bathroom cruelly revealed all the wrinkles I was used to blocking out in the soft light of my own bathroom mirror. On the last day, I was left in my hotel room without a call from him all morning. I was like a wild, caged animal, not knowing what to do with myself, not having a car or his daughter's number (we didn't have cell phones then). Finally, about noon, he showed up and said this wasn't working for him. I burst into tears, blaming myself for not even trying to seduce him the night before. When my plane landed in LA and I got to my car in the parking lot, I sat there with the windows up and wailed like Diane Keaton in *Something's Gotta Give* for almost an hour. Not since I was thrown out of Bhagwan's ranch had I felt this much pain from rejection. Unfortunately, my movie did not have a happy ending like Diane's. I think this was the final blow that ended any desire to actively search for a mate through the Internet.

My daughter, on the other hand, has had startling success, as she married the second guy she dated from Match.com. After celebrating six years together, it continues to be the perfect marriage. I was honored with an acknowledgment as her birth mom at the wedding reception and was also the official photographer.

I have been going through a lot of resistance to writing my last

Internet dating experience. I didn't want to remember it or talk about it until last night when I read a quote from the channeled book *I Am the Word* by Paul Selig that spoke directly to me: *"You are living the lives you have chosen and will continue to choose. And the creations you have created were all born in need. You needed them or you wouldn't have created them. We would like you each to see before you, in your mind's eye, your perfected self. We are before you leading the way, and we are behind you saying: 'Hurry, hurry, hurry. Go meet yourself. Go meet the beautiful self that you are and have always been.' You are merging now with your own vibration, the holiest self that you may know. Feel yourself in worth as you are engaged in marriage with your own Divine Self."*

PING! I pulled up to two women hugging on the sidewalk in front of the house, one with bags, indicating she was going to an airport. She was crying while the other tried to comfort her. The moment she got into the car and closed the door, she let out a full-blown heartbroken wail. She was a very attractive blond, but her makeup had become so smeared, she resembled a sad raccoon. She kept apologizing for crying, and I told her, "Please don't feel you have to apologize. Go ahead and just let it all hang out." She did and went through a handful of tissues. I asked her if she'd like to talk about it, and she immediately, between sobs, went into the whole story. It was about being rejected by a man that she had high hopes for while visiting here from Key West, Florida. She met him on an online dating service and spent about three weeks with him here in Northern California. They were so "into each other" they wasted no time renting a house to live in together. But she made the fatal mistake of "innocently" accepting a casual date for a drink with his best friend in hopes that he would join them both later. He went ballistic, misinterpreting her intentions, and no amount of rational explanations on her part could persuade him otherwise. Previously she had ignored all the red flags when he'd told her he had to have everything his way or not at all. The upshot: he kicked her out of the house in the meanest way possible and told her to never come back.

This so reminded me of me years ago. I tried to convince her that it was a good thing she found out now what he was like and that none of it was her fault. I told her she was a beautiful woman who deserved a lot better. She, of course, thought just like I did once, that it was all her fault and that she did something horribly wrong. By now I knew that with her state of mind, nothing I could say would make any difference. She was as determined as I once was to be the victim. When I told her that she was letting go of a toxic relationship so that she could make room for something better. She just gave me a blank stare. I changed the subject and asked her who her favorite movie star was, and she brightened and said, "Sofia Loren" and then thanked me for distracting her from her grief for a moment. (Sofia Loren? Really?)

This woman's pain and her complete submission into self-blame and victimhood reminded me so much of myself and all the years I suffered with this affliction. When I was thirteen years old, did I not proclaim that my greatest life goal was to love myself? As I near the end of this book, it is my fervent desire to reach this goal before the last page is scribed. This may be the ultimate purpose of writing my memoir.

24

IMAGINE

A Retirement Community of Loving Friends

For the first seven years of doing family beach portraits and children's vintage portraits from the end of 1997 to the beginning of 2004, my creative yearning was basically fulfilled.

But as usual, after seven years of doing one thing, restlessness set in, and my mind scoured the landscape for a new all-encompassing project. In 2004 I turned sixty-five, which is officially retirement age. Naturally, thoughts turned to the kind of life I would want or dream to have in retirement. I ultimately returned to the idea of communal living, of sorts, in a community of like minds and spirits, but with a twist: I wanted it to be a place where we owned or rented our own little houses but were connected to a main house where we could gather together for meals and movies or lectures if we wanted. I expanded the idea to include several in-house businesses operated by the members, such as an organic garden, a retreat center and spa, a wedding location, a publication house, an art studio and public art gallery, and a boutique selling our own flower essences, arts and crafts, and handmade jewelry. Far from being a retirement community, it would be a fully functional hub of creative activity and moneymaking businesses. I then added the idea of a health facility and assisted living for our aging members.

I began extensive computer research on existing co-housing communities, on building methods and materials, on design concepts, on environmental practices, and on building codes and land use laws in California, in other states, and in Mexico and Costa Rica. My favorite design concept was the Haiku house, which is a redwood structure with a clay tile roof topped with a skylight and a wraparound veranda. It's built on poles, allowing it to fit any terrain without needing a foundation. There were many designs and sizes to choose from. They would arrive in pieces by truck and require a construction crew to put together. Another favorite design was the underground "eggshell" houses that could escape the notice of aerial surveyors, if you couldn't find a location that would allow more than one structure per acre. I drew in a number of people who were interested, including Handy, who spent hours doing Internet research as well.

Several of us took trips to Mexico together to look over available property, but they were a little too remote, and the ride to them was unbearably unattractive because of the miles of garbage that lay rotting on the hillsides. We also took trips to Northern California and the Santa Cruz mountains in particular, because of the comparatively cheap land values there. We visited properties that already had structures and ones that didn't. I fell in love with a beautiful two-story home in Morgan Hill, which had a large pond and a big lawn area perfect for a retreat center and for weddings. The property extended into the forest behind and in front along the long drive to the house. I could see that dozens of cottages could be built along the creek behind the house.

I created a business plan that included this property and also a property in Southern California. My brother owned one hundred acres between Temecula and Warner Springs, and I was able to get him interested in letting us use his land if we would build a house for him and his wife and son away from the community up on the hill above. He was not interested in being a part of the community, as he is a very private person and has never been involved in any of the spiritual practices or teachings that I have embraced. A major drawback was the weather, which could reach up to 118 degrees in the summer. I designed a community of twenty-four houses on his property, ranging from Haiku pole houses to underground shell houses, which would be naturally cool in the summer and warm in winter. He had a natural spring and a pond area that was currently dry. Most of the one hundred acres were vertical, with about ten usable flatland acres.

One time, I traveled to Asheville, North Carolina, and met with a sannyasin real estate agent who showed me a few possibilities. I had never seen such a beautiful landscape of vine-covered trees and beautiful forests. But the humidity, and the strong stench of mold in every place I stayed, was a big deterrent.

PING! **Two middle-aged Mexican American women climbed in and were highly animated by the Hillary sticker I had on my bumper. One spoke robustly for the two of them and told me that she was doing everything she could to see that Hillary won. She and all her friends were very scared of Trump and had already begun to reap the consequences of the hate paranoia he had generated, as they experienced being demeaned by complete strangers every day. She said she'd like to tell them that she'd lived under a dictator, that they didn't know how good they had it in the US now, and what the consequences would be if they elected Trump. She spoke of the elections going on in Latin America and a deal she had made with her friends south of the border: if the liberal candidate won there, she would celebrate by eating their tacos, and if Hillary won here, she would invite them all for hamburgers.**

I'm still caught up in the political drama playing out on TV, and we are now only twenty-six days from the election. I've had many open discussions with my various Uber passengers, who all seem to be in agreement that Trump is despicable and has to go. This was even before the first debate, and then there was the Access Hollywood tape (i.e., sexual assault expose) and the second debate, which only compounded his unfitness for the office of president, causing prominent Republicans to leave in droves. Meanwhile, Russia and Wikileaks are furiously trying to balance the scales with their Clinton email exposés. Trump's hateful, demagogic rhetoric to his base is sickening, and now he's setting it up that if he loses, it's because the system is rigged. More than a million more guns have been sold since he began his campaign, and they talk incessantly about a revolution if he doesn't win. There have been many open threats by his supporters. It will be interesting to see what happens next.

I spent two years fully engaged in the creation of my Moonwater community, but to no avail. It was a wonderful dream, and still is, but with little prospect for actual manifestation. Like my Humanimal, it lay crumbled on a dusty road to nowhere.

25

THE GREATEST LOVE OF ALL
My Soul's Purpose Revealed

Meanwhile, my life as a photographer was creatively less and less fulfilling as I continued to do family portraits, professional head-shots, and vintage children's portraits. I joined more network groups to bolster my client base and became proficient at marketing my work through the personal contacts I made. But my "why" was missing. Who was I being other than a working photographer? Then one day an idea was presented to me that would be the answer to feeling more fulfilled. Someone told me I could work with teens at risk in lockup as a volunteer. It required a one-day training session, in which I would become a certified VIP (Volunteer in Probation).

I applied for the course, and after getting my certification, I chose to go to a lockup school in Santa Ana, where I could spend time with them in a schoolroom as an art teacher. My prior work as a social worker in LA and also as a district leader in the Buddhist organization prepared me to associate with them authentically and effectively. I visited the school for two hours, twice a week, and went home feeling energized, knowing I was making a difference in their lives. The one thing I noticed missing at the school was an element of love and respect for these kids. It seemed that so many on staff were in a punitive state of mind and very much on the same level of consciousness as the inmates themselves. So I did my best to show my appreciation for them as human beings and as potentially productive members of society. I would come up with a different art project every time and helped them to see life with new eyes.

One day, I had the idea to bring my camera, studio lighting equipment, a backdrop, and a rack of glamorous clothes and accessories for the girls to wear for a photo shoot. This was so much fun watching them "ooooh" and "aaaah" and support each other's experience of looking beautiful. After that, the girls received a free five-by-seven print of themselves.

There were several kids I became interested in: one in particular was a seventeen-year-old girl whose family lived in Laguna Niguel and who was in for heroin addiction. She was a repeat offender. Once she got out, she invariably hooked up with old friends who would drag her back into her addictive behavior, and she would end up either in juvenile hall or in the lockup school again. Several times she tearfully confided in me and expressed her despondency at being locked up.

I had her come to my studio, the first time she was out, and I dressed her in a red silk gown and did a classic portrait shoot, which helped me with my portfolio. She was naturally beautiful, with big brown Anne Hathaway eyes. It also helped her to see a side of herself she hadn't seen before. Another time I took her out on the streets of Laguna and did a series of black-and-white journalistic portraits, such as walking up a flight of stairs in a short, tight skirt and high heels, looking over her shoulder, carrying a boutique shopping bag; making a phone call in an iconic red British phone booth; and sitting on a park bench, smoking a cigarette and looking contemplative.

We became very close. She invited me to her house to meet her family. Once I took her to the emergency room at the local hospital to be checked for VD, which she suspected she had, and another time we went to the state fair in OC with a male friend of hers for a carefree, fun time. I lost touch with her after two years when I suspended my work at the school, but found out later that she was drug-free and had gotten a job with a law firm. This made me very happy.

PING! I was on the freeway heading toward Marin from Oakland when I got a call from the UC campus in Berkeley. Eloise, a woman of around fifty with long grayish-blond hair pulled back in a ponytail, entered my car with an overnight bag. I asked her if she was a student there, and she countered, "Oh, no, my daughter, Stacy, is. I was just helping her get settled into her new apartment." She showed me a picture of her on her iPhone.

I exclaimed, "She's beautiful. What is she majoring in?"

"Medicine, and to tell you the truth, this worries me."

"Why? Is she stressed out?"

"A little, but that's not the reason. Before coming to Berkeley, she was on Adderall for her ADHD condition. It's like crystal meth, you know. Her father is the one who thought it was a good idea to take Adderall so she could focus on her studies. He's always pushing her to excel at everything. She listens to him because he's paying the bills.

"She told me she finally got off it, but occasionally has been using marijuana and other recreational drugs. She insists she's not addicted and can stop anytime she decides to. But meeting her new roommates, who have tattoos, pierced lips, and purple hair, I worry that she's not in the best company to manage her 'non'-addictions. She has a cousin who is only seventeen and is in a rehab center for heroin."

I asked, "Why does her studying medicine worry you?"

She said, "Because she'll have easy access to all of that stuff when she's a doctor."

I surmised, "Well, that's a long way off, and by then she may have grown out of the need or desire for it."

"That's true. I guess I'm really more worried about the drug culture now at Berkeley and wondering if I can have a positive enough influence on her from four hundred miles away, for her to make the right choices. It's just so scary, and I feel so helpless to do anything about it. I'm always walking a fine line with her, trying not to put her off with any lectures or even suggestions."

I exclaimed, "It must be hard being a mom, especially one with a brilliant and independently willful child. My kudos to you. I can't imagine what it would be like to care so much for someone and not be able to stop them from making bad choices. Addiction is so insidious. It's always, 'Just one more time won't hurt.'"

Quietly she murmured, "I know." I looked through my rearview mirror and saw her head bowed and a tear running slowly down one cheek. Quickly, she brushed it aside and smiled, asking, "Do you have any kids?" I told her my story and felt as though I had just made a friend I could reveal everything to. She listened with genuine interest, although she had every reason to be absorbed in her own thoughts and not hear a word I said. When I finally dropped her off at the airport, I got out of the car and gave her a big hug and my card, asking her to please feel free to call anytime. I then turned off my Uber app and headed home in silence and said a prayer for this brave woman and her beautiful daughter.

PING! Several months later I had a chance encounter with a young woman named Stacy and her boyfriend, Tony. I was driving around Berkeley when I got the call to pick them up and take them to an Ethiopian restaurant in downtown Oakland. She looked vaguely familiar. I wondered if we had ever met. It was when she ran her fingers through her hair, laughing at something Tony said, that I remembered the photo of her by the woman I'd picked up months earlier named Eloise. What synchronicity! I was reminded of my special prayer for the day, which was "to be of service in a new and unexpected way." I told her about the ride with her mother, and she shouted, "No way!" She went on to say that she had just called her mom to tell her that she had decided to drop out of med school and pursue biological ecology instead and was very happy. She stated she loved plants and animals more than she loved humans and wanted to do her part in helping save the planet. Tony was studying to be a nutritionist, and they both seemed really connected and passionate about their life goals. There was no sign of anything off or unnatural about them. I decided to find the card Eloise left me and give her an encouraging call when I got home (which I did, and we've been good friends ever since).

Another opportunity for my purpose of empowering women and guiding them toward self-love first appeared around 2005 when a friend introduced me to *kirtan*, which is a traditional East Indian musical meditation practice. A group of about fifteen of us, mostly women between forty-five and sixty and a couple of millennials, met every Wednesday morning in the sanctuary of the Neighborhood Congregational Church and sang our hearts out. Having lost most of my midrange vocal cords to Buddhist chanting years ago, I sang harmony in the baritone range. I also got really good at playing the djembe drum and became the official creator and keeper of the beat.

One day, one of my closest friends there announced the arrival of *Ashes and Snow* in Santa Monica. It was a huge traveling photo and video show displaying peaceful interactions between humans and wild animals within a uniquely designed Nomadic Museum. She was ecstatic about it. I booked a ticket, and my life literally changed after seeing it for myself. I was sixty-seven at the time and was contemplating retirement. But when I saw this, a bold proclamation escaped my lips: "I'm not done yet!" I left the exhibition with mascara tears streaming down my cheeks. Gregory Colbert had nailed it! Being from Canada, he had spent eight years traveling the world to film every major wild beast on land, air, and sea, interacting with temple dancers, underwater dancers, child monks, and wise old meditators. He documented the mutual love and respect that can be attained between man and beast, and he did so with artistic acumen unlike anything I'd ever seen. I was inspired not only by the subject matter but also by his sepia-toned, dreamlike photographic style. There was a deeply spiritual and ethereal tone throughout the exhibition. This was a turning point for me. His work can be seen at www.gregorycolbert.com.

The next time I went to kirtan, I noticed how exquisitely beautiful the women were in their colorful and exotic East Indian dress. In my mind I saw them singularly or together, meditating or dancing on the beach by the water's edge. So that following Saturday, I had nine of these women in full Eastern Indian–wear gather at the beach at eight in the morning. Thus began my new career of photographing women over forty as "the Natural Goddess." My first ever goddess photo was taken by my assistant from atop a lifeguard station, looking down at nine of us lying in a circle with the top of our heads facing a gold plate of roses in the center. Our hands were in a prayer, or Namaste, mudra. Inspired by *Ashes and Snow*, I desaturated the color on most all of the portraits, giving them a tinge of color, like my hand-colored vintage film portraits of children. By this time, I had finally transitioned from film to digital photography and had become proficient with Photoshop tools.

I felt a strong calling to empower women over forty with my god-dess portraits. It was apparent to me that in all my family portraits, most women considered themselves less important in the portrait than their children or even their husbands. I also noticed that women over forty needed reassurance that they were still beautiful and desir-able enough to be competitive with younger women in securing a life partner or to keep an existing marriage from falling apart. I dabbled in boudoir portraiture but did not feel that these were authentic rep-resentations of women's true beauty and grace. Taking them out of the studio against canvas backdrops and placing them in nature in flowing gowns and scarves, I saw them come alive and be transformed into goddesses. Much like the women in Colbert's photos, who were meditating with cheetahs or dancing in the water with elephants, a spirit emerged that far transcended anything captured in a glamour photo. Women have a symbiotic relationship with nature that brings out her true sexuality and beauty. I wanted women to have the opportunity to see that in themselves through these portraits.

I collected dozens of gowns and accessories from secondhand stores and a couple hundred yards of different-colored silk fabric for scarves and photographed hundreds of women in various locations as goddesses during the next ten years. The first year I created a group of twenty images that I regarded as gallery-worthy and presented them to Reverend Michael Beckwith at the Agape International Spiritual Center in Culver City. I had been a regular member of that congregation for almost eighteen years. He agreed to let me display my work for six weeks in the halls leading to the sanctuary. They also gave me a space for an outdoor exhibit to market my portraiture to the thousands of members in between services. Thus my goddess portrait business expanded exponentially, and the makings of a book began to take shape as well.

Over the next several years I photographed many beautiful women over forty, and the ones I thought were the best representation of my art and the purpose of the book I asked for a personal story of an epiphany or transformational experience. For those who weren't able to write a story, I inserted a poem from Rumi, Kahlil Gibran, Maya Angelou, and several others. Marianne Williamson agreed to let me use three of her quotes from *A Woman's Worth*. I also wrote my own poetry whenever inspired by a photo. So this was not only a book of beautiful photos; it contained messages of encouragement from women over forty to other women facing challenging circumstances in their lives.

PING! **Pulling up to a cottage in Mill Valley, I waited for my rider. After a few minutes, Georgia, a stunning blond woman in a black leather dress, appeared with a briefcase and handbag. As soon as she got in the car, she opened her case, which doubled as a cosmetics case, and began her twenty-five-minute transformation** (the exact amount of time it took to drive to San Francisco). At first there were few words between us, until she blurted out, "Are you an artist?"

Shocked, I replied, "Yes, a photographer."

She said I reminded her of her mother, who was also an artist. Then we began an animated conversation about her livelihood, which was as an art dealer, beginning successfully years ago with photographic works by Ansel Adams and branching out to paintings and sculptures. I told her that she herself looked like a painting, and I would have enjoyed using her as a model, with or without makeup. She laughed and thanked me for the compliment as she gathered her things to leave. Georgia was so grounded in her identity; she really needed no affirmation of her self-worth.

The following pair of riders from Los Angeles was in stark contrast, reminding me of the "looking good" culture I left in Southern California for the more spiritual and ecological culture here in the Bay Area. I had come to the conclusion soon after I moved here that my goddess portrait business was doomed, because women here were just not into glorifying their looks for posterity like they were in LA, Orange, and San Diego Counties. I guess being close to the entertainment industry has a more direct effect on women's self-image. "Looking good" notwithstanding, I, at least, gave women in Southern California a deeper experience of themselves in nature through my photography.

By 2007 I brought a sample book of *The Natural Goddess* to Agape when Marianne Williamson was speaking there. I handed her my book, and she gave me an endorsement. Later that same year, I acquired a literary agent named Devra Jacobs, who had some movie industry connections, which she gave to me in hopes of soliciting them for photo shoots for my book. Her reasoning was simple: I was an unknown author, and this was an expensive full-color coffee-table book to pitch to publishers. Having well-known celebrities featured in the book might give her the leverage she needed to sell the book. Meanwhile, I sought out other celebrities through attending women's conferences where they were speaking. I went up to Stefanie Powers, Mariel Hemingway, and Marla Maples and successfully talked them into doing a shoot. My agent introduced me to Diane Ladd; Connie Stevens; and Brit Elders, the CEO and best friend of Shirley MacLaine.

Brit, Devra, and I had high hopes for Shirley, and she was definitely interested and willing, but about that time her career sprang into new life, and she was in one film after another, ending up in the UK on *Downton Abbey*. Also Mariel had agreed, but when we scheduled a shoot, she had to cancel because of work that came up, and later she employed a new assistant who was not aware of our previous connection and blocked me from reaching Mariel again. Another star I had contacted was Lainie Kazan, who was very interested and excited, but one shoot after another was scheduled and canceled because of a cold, then a sprained ankle, and twice for work-related issues.

I enjoyed my brief relationships with Mariel and Lainie and was disappointed that we couldn't make it happen. Lainie invited me to watch her perform at a club in Hollywood, and I was so taken with her powerful sultry voice and the fact that she had been a stand-in for Barbara Streisand on Broadway. Her most recent work was as the mother of the bride in *My Big Fat Greek Wedding*. What I loved about Mariel was her dedication to growing organic food, keeping fit in body, mind, and spirit, and spending time in nature—and her gorgeous long legs.

I was honored to photograph Diane Ladd twice at her beautiful estate in Ojai. When Devra first introduced me to her, Diane invited me to a fundraiser she was having at her home, and she included my offer of a goddess portrait by displaying one of my framed portraits and auctioning off a sitting by me. She introduced me to many of the stars there, including her daughter Laura Dern, along with Valerie Harper and Della Reese. I reintroduced myself to Larry Hagman, with whom I had worked on *Dallas* forty years ago. He was still the spit-fire character he played on *Dallas*. A month later I came back with my assistant and some gowns and shawls for Diane to wear as we explored all the possibilities for portraits on her rambling estate. I returned again for some personal PR shots of her in street clothes inside her home. She turned out to be a champion of my work, and we have been in communication by phone from time to time since then. I find her to be highly spiritual and an activist for human rights.

I photographed Connie Stevens in her spacious backyard in Bel-Air. My afternoon with her was delightful, starting with doing her makeup and hair and selecting her wardrobe in her boudoir next to her bedroom and study. She had been living in this classic mansion with her daughters since the sixties, when she was in her prime and married to Eddie Fisher. My makeup girl commented on the supple-ness of her skin at age seventy-two and believed she hadn't had any cosmetic procedures done to her face or neck. Perhaps it was because of her successful line of anti-aging creams called Forever Spring that she was able to retain the freshness of youth.

That same year, I photographed Marla Maples with her best friend, Tara Sutphen, a well-known psychic in Hollywood. We picked out a great location at Rocky Oaks Park in the Malibu mountains. At the time, Marla wasn't that well known, except for the fact that she was a beauty queen and once had been married to Donald Trump.

Turns out, not only is she beautiful, but she is highly spiritual, with her own group of spiritual sisters. For one shot, she climbed up a tree in her form-fitting blue silk dress and reclined on a branch while Tara stood below her, leaning against the trunk. Marla said she used to be a tomboy and loved climbing trees. Now that Trump is in the news every day, she has also been featured on many talk shows, including *Oprah* and *The View*, and in a few TV documentaries about Trump.

Other stars and celebrities I photographed were Stefanie Powers,

Barbara Marx Hubbard, Terry Cole-Whittaker, Arielle Ford, and Lynn Andrews.

My experience with Barbara Marx Hubbard was particularly memorable. Her portrait was done in a park across the street from her home in Santa Barbara. I brought her a long red satin Mandarin dress, which she loved and looked stunning in. We walked to the park, and when we landed on the perfect spot surrounded by flowers and trees, she stood there majestically and stated, "I feel like Eve in the Garden of Co-Creation." One passerby commented on how beautiful she was and thought it must be her excellent bone structure. I knew it was her natural radiance that created that impression. She was seventy-nine.

My day with Terry Cole-Whittaker in Temescal Canyon near Brentwood also stood out. It was filled with magic and laughter. She was like a little girl delighting in being out in nature, dressed in her fancy long velvet duster, matching culottes, and gold sandals. She spoke of her many experiences beyond the veil with her spirit guides. At one point, her age came up, and she proudly announced that she was sixty-nine and a half as if she couldn't wait to be seventy. She had been a spiritual icon in the eighties with her own TV ministry and is still very active with speaking engagements nationwide.

PING! Samantha, a very attractive Cameron Diaz look-alike, entered my car. I started a conversation by asking how long she had been living in San Francisco, and she said five years but was ready to move on as she'd just broke up with her five-year relationship. I remarked, "Five years is a long time for a relationship."

She said, "Yes, but he is an idiot" and then added, "All men are idiots."

I agreed to that and added, "Well, there are different levels of idiocy, and now perhaps you're ready for the next level up."

She laughed and said, "That would be nice, but for now I would like to move to London, or as far away from San Francisco as possible."

She seemed like a woman fully in her power. There was not a hint of depression or self-pity in her response, merely a longing for a new adventure. Her level of self-worth became really apparent when she told me about her college experience. I opened up about having gone to UC Berkeley and being admitted only because my father and grandfather were alums, not because of my grades. Thoughtfully, she said, "Well, you could have gone somewhere else."

I countered with "Yes, but I was rejected." She giggled and then said she had been rejected too, from University of San Diego.

Now, here is the interesting part: she told me that instead of accepting the rejection, she sent a letter to appeal that decision. A letter came back declining an appeal, so she decided to meet with them in person and put forth her case. She understood that nothing might come of it, but she had to at least give it a try or never know what could have been possible. Of course, when they met, they were so impressed by her audacious determination they devised a plan which would allow her to attend as a full student the following semester. I told her that she was a girl after my own heart and that my work was all about women's empowerment and that I would love to tell her story in my book.

26

WHAT A FEELING

I Took My Passion and Made It Happen

Still focused on women's empowerment, in 2008 I wrote a screenplay called *The Lady in the Jewel Box* about a magical jewel box that appears in five vignettes featuring disillusioned and estranged women over forty. Inside the jewel box are mystical messages reminding them of their original dreams and goals in life to inspire them to do a reset. I wrote a nine-minute trailer and set about campaigning for funds at CEO Space. I managed to raise enough to satisfy the needs of a production company I found within that organization. I set up auditions in my studio and also looked for mother and daughter look-alikes on the Internet for a time-lapse sequence about a teenage ballerina who gave up her dream in order to get married and who finds herself unhappy and unfulfilled at forty.

After deciding on our free non-equity actors (big mistake, I realized later), we used familiar locations in Laguna Beach. I was lucky to be in communication with Dannion Brinkley and his co-author wife, Kathryn, who is a dark-haired beauty, and their look-alike teenage daughter, Adriana. They agreed to be in the first vignette and came to Laguna for their one day out of the two-day shoot. Our beach scene was rather dicey, as we didn't have a permit to film there, and the lifeguard came over to inquire as to what we were doing. There were at least sixteen people making up the crew, actors, and family members, as well as all the lighting and sound equipment. Dannion came to the rescue with an ingenious explanation: he told the lifeguard that a woman's child had died and that we were doing a video in homage to her child. (We had a child actor in the scene.) From that time forward, filming went on without a hitch for two days. The biggest thing that came of this was an invaluable learning experience that will be useful if I ever intend to write another screenplay and film another trailer.

PING! I pulled up to a nice house in Novato, and Talia, an attractive young black woman with a tint of red in her multi-braided hair, appeared with a suitcase, escorted by an older guy and his four-year-old daughter. He put the suitcase in the back, they said their goodbyes, and then she got in the front and waved goodbye to the child. She was an au pair from Johannesburg, South Africa, who had just been fired. She was in tears, saying she'd made a horrible decision that cost her the job after only two weeks. I was to drive her to Oakland, where she would be staying with someone from the agency until she could find another au pair job. Moments before I picked her up, I said my prayer and declared that I would be a positive influence on someone today. I managed to say all the right things that gave her comfort and ease and then told her about my prayer. She slapped her knee and said, "This is a miracle from God. Thank you! I feel so much better. If you had been anyone else, I would still be crying and feeling like my life was worthless." I didn't ask her what happened, as I felt she would tell me in time, which she did.

She tentatively broached the subject, saying she'd made the mistake of having a drink of wine at eleven in the morning while the child was at school and then felt she had to be honest and tell the parents. That caused them to think she was an alcoholic, having wine so early in the day, and decided to let her go. She knew she did the wrong thing and said this was a pattern of self-sabotage she was very familiar with in her life. To me, she was very self-observant and wise for a girl just out of high school. She told me her big dream was to be an actress in live theater and to be a professional singer. I automatically went into a monologue about my life and was able to impart some wisdom that may help steer her in the right direction in that extremely misogynistic and vulnerable vocation. When we arrived at her destination, I gave her my phone number and told her to call anytime she needed someone to talk to.

In lieu of a failed attempt at making a movie to empower women, I came up with the idea of creating a Festival of Goddesses in Laguna Beach in 2009. I envisioned a full day of speeches and panel discussions by role-model women around feminine issues and live music, ecstatic dancing, catered food, boutique vendors, and a fashion show. I decided to add one important element: handsome male servers to honor the women as goddesses. This proved to be very transforming for both the men and the women.

Our first festival, in 2010, was held in Bridge Hall at the Neighborhood Congregational Church with over one hundred in attendance and was so well received that the following year we decided to expand to the Festival of Arts grounds, which can hold up to one thousand people with spaces for 180 vendors. It also includes a theater house with a seating capacity of 230. This was a huge undertaking and required a full year of planning and soliciting enough vendors and possible sponsors up front to pay for the venue. We expanded the program for both 2011 and 2012 to include a full day of live entertainment on the grounds, along with ecstatic (free-form) dancing, a fashion show, and a silent auction. Inside the theater we had four panel discussions by well-known authors on women's issues and later a video of men making heartfelt apologies to the female gender for all their transgressions. After the video, we invited the men in the audience to come up to the front and make their own apologies. There was not a dry eye in the house as the men themselves broke down and cried while apologizing for their own bad behavior toward women. Each festival ended with a kirtan concert by Larisa Stow and Shakti Tribe in the theater, which rocked with high vibrations.

We lost money the first year at that venue with only three hundred or so in attendance, but we gained a reputation that brought a breakthrough turnout and success the following year. The following year we broke even and expanded on everything and also brought in Laura's House, a safe house for abused women, as our live auction charity project.

I was exhausted after three full years of planning and producing these festivals. Although we were successful, I personally had no income after expenses from the event. I decided to pull out and either sell it to another event producer or let someone on the team take over. After a few people showed interest but not enough to buy, the festival became just another beautiful memory. However, it's quite possible it will be resurrected in this age of #MeToo, as I've heard from quite a few women wishing for it to happen again.

For now, it's clear that my successes aren't measured quantifiably in dollars but in the quality of personal impacts on people's lives. It's also clear that I'm not done yet.

During that time, I had no interest in the opposite sex, as I was driven and focused primarily on the festival for three consecutive years. Consequently, my pheromones were not activated, and there was nothing and no one to distract me from my purpose.

27

FINDING MY WAY BACK HOME
Who Knew It Would Be in Marin?

With the completion of the 2012 Festival of Goddesses, it was time to pull my *Natural Goddess* book off the shelf and finish it. At the same time, my landlord suggested I start looking for another place to live, as they were now contemplating selling the duplex and/or raising the rent. They said the rent would go up one thousand dollars, so they left me no choice but to move. I had lived there eighteen years, with Hercules seventeen of those years, and in Laguna altogether for twenty-eight years.

My dear friend and soul sister VJ, an Ayurvedic doctor who lived next door to me in Laguna, drove up the coast to Ukiah with me for a wedding. We stopped at the Good Earth market and café in Fairfax on the way. There I had a revelation that Marin was to be my new home. She had the same idea, as she comes there once a month for certain clients. We were giddy with excitement over our mutual decision to move up there. We spent the next month scouring the Internet for available houses for rent and drove up once to check out two or three we liked. We came to the conclusion that we should go our separate ways since I had a cat, which she could not see as a fit for her lifestyle. As luck would have it, I found the perfect one-bedroom granny apartment in Novato, just fifteen minutes north of San Rafael. She found a small apartment for almost nothing in a friend's house in Corte Madera. This allowed her to keep her place in Laguna as well, but she didn't move in until three or four months later.

What followed, exactly four years ago, was having a huge garage sale, packing a large truck and my car with Hercules on board, and driving to our new location in Novato. Before leaving, I went to my last kirtan with my friends in Laguna and was honored with a farewell celebration and a new djembe drum of my own. I had been drumming and singing every week with them for over ten years. I broke down and cried when we sang a Sufi song to each other called "All I Ask of You Is to Always Remember Me as Loving You." I realized then the full extent of what I had chosen to do by leaving Laguna forever. VJ was in this group as one of the lead singers.

Hercules and I crossed the Richmond Bridge around 7:30 p.m. and saw a very unusual cloud formation, like one long tube across the entire sky. I have never seen such a phenomenon before or since. After meeting my really wonderful landlords and settling in, my first inclination was to explore the area and hike some of the many beautiful forested trails. My next task was to meet as many people as possible and begin to form a new tribe in Marin.

First stop was the MLK gym in Sausalito on Sunday mornings, where there is an 8:30 a.m. and an 11 a.m. Sweat Your Prayers ecstatic dance meditation with 150 participants in each session. I connected with one guy in particular, named David, who turned out to be the perfect connector to dozens of Marin's finest. He and his wife Andrea invited me to a Jewish Shabbat at their home, where I met some of the people I would be hanging with in the future. I found that many, like me, were gentile but resonated with their Jewish friends.

I was never exposed to anything remotely Jewish until I was on my own and was employed in the garment industry and later in showbiz. But even then, I never attended a Hanukah celebration or a Bar Mitzvah and had never even heard of a Shabbat. But I have to say my

father and everyone on his side look extremely Jewish. In his despera-
tion to hide the fact, my father even had a nose job done in the sixties
because some people had commented that he looked Jewish because
of his big nose. I imagine his fear of looking Jewish came from the
impact World War II had on him when he joined the army.

When VJ moved to Marin, I was able to introduce her to some
of my new friends. She also had a few of her own, and we often took
trips to Sonoma for shopping and café breaks or hung out at various restaurants, including the Sweetwater Restaurant and Bar in Mill
Valley, where dance bands played and we danced. Often, there were
one or two of our friends from SoCal visiting and joining us in our
Bay Area adventures.

PING! Three forty-something women piled into my car and were
in high gear—highly animated, very chatty, and very loud, trying
to outdo each other in rhapsodic exclamations. They were going to
a Dave Matthews concert at the Greek Theater in Berkeley, which
meant I would be trapped in my car with them for the next hour or
so. Sometimes I'm in their kind of a mood, and sometimes I'm not.
This was one of those "not" moments. I was in more of a Yo-Yo Ma
mood, but you don't get to choose your riders. So I zoned out at first,
just focusing on the flow of traffic and putting the chitchat noise in
the background of my mind. Eventually their energy began to seep
through my self-imposed wall, and I started to relate to them in an
open and friendly way. They reminded me of *Sex in the City*, and I
secretly attributed a certain character from that series to each one.
At the end of the ride, the Carrie Bradshaw character said she would
give me a five-star rating. I felt amply rewarded.

VJ and I also took long walks on trails in Mill Valley and Novato
and had in-depth conversations, mostly about her relationships with
men. Not only was VJ inherently wise and together as a woman, she
was a stunning blond with extremely good taste in clothes and interior décor. She had a propensity for gray and white in both areas. I

admired her casually elegant style and later took on her example by supplying my closet with numerous gray-and-white outfits. She had a white Prius, and I later bought a white Prius.

I refused to believe that I had given my power away until one day I realized that I had. It reminded me of my time decades earlier with Patti and Dick. So *BAM*, without thinking, I emailed a long goodbye letter to her saying I needed to find my own center away from her for a while, as I felt she didn't support me emotionally and that all the focus was on her. This erupted into a vicious email battle back and forth until she slammed the door shut on our relationship forever. I was devastated. I couldn't believe what I had done to myself again, only this time with a soul sister.

With only two more years left to talk about, I realize that perhaps I may not reach my goal of unconditional self-love before the last chapter. Realistically, it may take a major satori (spiritual awakening) or many more lifetimes. However, there's always a possibility that a Hollywood ending could show up, but I'm not sure that is what this book is about.

Besides working on the publication of my first book, my time in Marin has been embellished with the inclusion of a weekly book club for *A Course in Miracles* and other like-minded books channeled by ascended masters—most notably, the *I Am the Word* series by Paul Selig. I have found this to be one of the most profound, life-changing teachings I have experienced.

My prayer of intention originated from this book, and when I recite it every day before driving, it helps me to remember who I really am as an aspect of the Creator and that everyone we encounter are likewise aspects of God. One of my closest friends in the group has done a 180-degree flip from being a pushover for men who would exploit her sexually to finally being in a healthy, mutually loving relationship at the age of sixty-four. *The Word* has also given me a fresh new perspective of who I am, and it shows up with the warm, loving friendships I'm enjoying in my new community as well as with my fabulous Uber passengers.

However, I have not gone to a meeting in over four months because it's always on a Friday night, which is my biggest Uber driving time besides Saturday evening. Lately I have been feeling called to come back, and a series of events took place that drove that thought home. I was driving a client on Magnolia in Corte Madera and suddenly noticed that the license plate of the car in front of me read, "I AM WORD." I wanted to honk and pull the woman over, but I had a paying passenger and couldn't. The car was in front of me for a good twenty minutes. I couldn't shake her, couldn't pass or turn as we both were going in the same direction on a two-lane street. I later discovered the owner of that car is the woman who transcribed Paul Selig's *I Am Word* books.

Two days later I picked up a passenger in Sausalito who was headed for the bus station in San Francisco, and I noticed he had beautiful eyes like Osho and told him so. He said, "Oh, I've read many of his books. But the book I'm reading now by Paul Selig called *I Am the Word* has really impacted me powerfully."

I said, "You're kidding!'" and inwardly I groaned, *OK, God, I get it. You want me to go back to the book club.* So I made the commitment to go that Friday evening. On Friday afternoon, I turned on my app to see how much I had earned so far that week, knowing it had been a very light week and would be lighter still with no Friday earnings. It so happened I'd received a six-hundred-dollar bonus for referring someone to be a driver, whose name I did not recognize and didn't remember ever referring. All my defenses were down. I couldn't back out now.

Besides feeling a strong connection to Source when reading the book aloud in the group, I've discovered it is a powerful way to know others and to know ourselves more deeply in relation to others. I feel blessed being in this process of evolvement with such a beautiful group of people.

PING! A stocky LGBT woman of about seventy entered my car, and immediately I recognized her as the facilitator of *A Course in Miracles* when I took it two years ago. I remembered her as brilliant, knowing how to direct the discussion and being on point with her interpretation of the text. It was truly an honor to be her Uber driver that day. I told her I was on my last chapter of my book and that I had just written about the course—and here she was in my car! She laughed and said, "There are no accidents!"

I blithely remarked, "That's good to know, so now I can drive you to your destination with that in mind." We both laughed, and it was good seeing her again.

I think the main objective of these book clubs is to get together with others in a meaningful way and to express ourselves more openly and affirmatively. The exchange of ideas and the sharing of one's life experiences as they relate to the teachings are invigorating and not only bring us closer to an understanding of ourselves but help to build friendships. Many times, during the discussions at the book clubs, we have great "aha" moments that are momentary and fleeting but, taken together over a certain period of time, may bring us to a lasting transcendence. I've noticed a significant rise in the vibration at the meetings after being away for several months. Certain individuals seemed to have attained a higher level of awareness and ability to articulate their newly found wisdom.

I also noticed a new feeling of belonging and expressions of admiration and love being directed my way by everyone there. Perhaps my using the proclamations of "I am the Word" and "I know who I am" as an Uber driver has raised my vibration as well. In essence I am affirming divine self-love every day. Could it be I am closer to my goal than I thought?

28

BE

A Light unto Yourself

A huge turning point occurred last year when I drove home from a trip to Laguna to find my beloved Hercules in critical condition from a failing heart. He was twenty years old and my best buddy, my baby. I knew he wasn't well, but he was stable and being taken care of by two wonderful women, so I took a chance and went to Laguna for a few days, which I had been planning for over a month. I told him to please wait for me. On my third day there, I suddenly felt that I had to go home, and so I left a day early. Sure enough, he was panting, unable to breathe normally. He let out a soft cry as I kissed him and held him close and then took him to the pet hospital. Hours after giving him oxygen and a shot to clear his lungs, he hadn't gotten any better. They sadly informed me that there was nothing left but to put him down to relieve him of his suffering. His time had come. At 4:40 a.m. on July 17, I held him in my arms as they delivered the serum through an IV. It didn't hit me until I got home that he was truly gone from my life forever.

Four years ago he had been diagnosed with lymphoma and had only three months to live. Somehow I was able to save him through the laying on of hands each time he had episodic bouts of the sickness. I concentrated with all my might on sending healing energy into his body. The fifth time I gave him my "Super Love" energy, he jumped up and was never sick from cancer again. I think we are all capable of healing our loved ones if we truly believe it. This reminds me of when I was nine years old, obsessed with acquiring three new dresses. With that same high level of intention and belief, I was able to transform reality. I also remember how it felt to walk on burning coals. I tell people that after some mental preparation using chants and prayers, when my time came, it felt like walking on Styrofoam popcorn. No one, including myself, suffered the slightest burn. That experience reminded me of how powerful the mind is and how anything is possible. But still, why haven't I been able to apply that kind of energy to manifesting a relationship?

My laying on of hands didn't work this time. I somehow knew it was his time and couldn't change that. Heartbroken, I cried that whole day, feeling the emptiness in my house. None of the reassuring sounds he made were there to remind me of his loving presence. I no longer woke up with his whiskers tickling my nose or his wet nose poking my closed eye with a lick or two. However, the next morning I awoke at five with a loud purring in my ear. I turned and patted the bed beside me to see if anything was there. Nothing. When I awoke later, I suddenly felt as if all sadness had been washed away. I was perfectly normal and couldn't believe it, so I tried recalling the most poignant memories of him, and it felt as though I had been anesthetized. The memories were like a faded photograph and had no effect on my emotions. This was a miracle, and I knew that he had somehow healed my grief, possibly as payback for the time I healed him or, more probably, because of our unconditional love for each other. He is in my heart forever.

This had to have been the ultimate test. Take away the only object of affection left in my life and see how I manage my emotions. At first I struggled and felt desperate to find a replacement. After two failed attempts to adopt a cat, I finally just let it go. Now it doesn't seem to

matter if I get another cat or dog or not. I feel the same about a relationship. The door is open and the welcome mat is out, but the table is
set for only one at the moment. To be honest, my longing for compan-
ionship has been diminished almost to the point of nonexistence, as I
get so much juice every day with my friends and Uber connections. I
meet the most extraordinary people who inspire me.

Also, I have to admit with some hesitation that the thing that has
stopped me from actively searching for an intimate relationship at
my age is noticing how my physical body seems to be rapidly deteri-
orating. I have unattractive age spots creeping up my arms and legs
and face; thinning hair; many more wrinkles on my face (where is
that guy who offered to pay for a facelift?); a bloated belly; and skin
keratosis on my back, which the dermatologist calls old-age barnacles.
I couldn't help thinking it would be a challenge for anyone to want
to make love to this grossly flawed physical representation of me. As
an artist, it's always been difficult to separate myself from the beauty
standards that I apply to everyone else.

Anyway, I've come to the place where I don't think my self-love
depends on my opinion of my physical image. I can now look into
the mirror and say, "It is what it is. So what? And hey, I'm not so bad
for an old broad!" However, it is a blessing that I'm not aware of how
I look most of the time, since I don't go around holding a mirror in
front of me everywhere. My true mirrors are in the eyes of the people
I meet each day. They tell me I am beautiful and loved. Over time I
have learned to be true to myself, to stand up for my truth and kindly
reject any opposition to it. I also know I am not my body, given my
three out-of-body experiences. Ultimately, I believe self-love comes
from knowing that I am a child of God and therefore loved by Him/
Her unconditionally and forever, even when I'm wrong or untrue to
myself.

**_PING!_ It was Mother's Day, and I decided to work the early day
shift instead of the early evening shift. I picked a rose and put it in**

a small water bottle to mark the occasion. After driving two separate mothers with their loving husbands and children in tow, I was summoned by four gay Salvadoran guys in San Francisco who wanted to celebrate the bright sunny day at the Presidio. Their plan was to take selfies and pictures of the coastline and the Golden Gate Bridge and send them to their mothers in San Salvador. When they entered the car, their cologne engulfed the car's interior, overtaking the scent of the rose. But mostly, their friendly jubilance permeated the car with high energy and laughter.

Two of them spoke enough English to enable me to interact with them. I asked if they were going to celebrate with their mothers, and they sadly said no, that they wished they could, but that their *madres* were in San Salvador. I asked how they liked living in San Francisco, and they brightened up noticeably and in unison exclaimed, "Oh *sí*, we love it here. We are *free* to be ourselves and to live unashamed of who we are. No one here judges us or condemns us for being gay." There was lively chitchat in both English and Spanish after that, and when I delivered them to their destination, one of them gave me a five-dollar tip, and they all smiled broadly as they waved goodbye. It was a perfect ending for my Uber adventures that day.

Here is the perfect message from God to me: "There is no need, my dearest friend, to love yourself, not from the level of the divided mind, the ego. For all of this is a fantasy. There is nothing else that is needed, only the celebration of your Love, and the moments for remembering the truth." —*The Messages from God* through Yael and Doug Powell AMEN!

So now that that's settled and self-love is a done deal, what do I do about my elusive soul mate? Surely now is the opportune time for him to show up, right? As much as I thought my desire for a relationship was diminished by my consumptive creativity, I realized I might be fooling myself a little. My creative outlets were the excuse I always used to justify my aloneness to myself and to curtail any moments of depression that crept in when thinking about it.

So, I took a deep breath and decided to be proactive by enrolling in a seven-week course by Katherine Woodward Thomas called *Calling in the One*, which I understood had a high success rate for attracting and having a long-term intimate relationship with your soul mate. I had to push past my built-in skepticism from years of failing so many workshops on this subject.

The first week of the course was an introduction and an overview of what to expect along with seven days of exercises and meditations to increase our awareness of ourselves and the people around us. Each week had a specific course of action toward our personal growth with seven days of exercises and meditations. By the end of the second week, I began to notice a shift in my consciousness. I no longer clung to my "ironclad" sad story. . . . It seemed over-rehearsed. Although it elicited the same expressions of sympathy from everyone in the group, it strangely rang hollow to me. It frankly surprised me that, after more than forty-five years of meditation and grueling, hard transformational work, anything new could have such an effect on me. When I began, I was positive I had done it all and this was just going to be a reminder. But by the third and fourth week, I realized this was different. I found myself deeply engaged and awestruck by so many new revelations. By the fifth week I suddenly got the brilliant idea to focus with all my might on a prayer of intention, like I did when I was nine or when I healed Hercules and, to a lesser extent, like I do every day as an Uber driver.

My prayer felt really powerful as I spread my request far and wide over the treetops and mountains and oceans to the starry reaches of the universe.

A side note: During this course I noticed a strange phenomenon while driving. It seemed every day I was either surrounded by sleek Tesla cars or sapphire-blue cars of any make or model. I had never seen a sapphire-blue Tesla, so I made it up that when I actually saw a sapphire-blue Tesla, my true love would appear in my life.

Before I got to Chapter 6 of the course and just after I said my prayer, a sapphire-blue Tesla appeared coming out of the Whole Foods Market as I was going in. The driver's eyes met mine and smiled, and I suddenly realized what I was looking at.

29

HALLELUJAH
Says It All

My love of self has finally taken hold, and life is a song of continuous celebration, more like a Bollywood movie than an American B-movie with a predictable ending. Life is still a mystery but not a dilemma or a drama anymore. There may be a few pieces of the puzzle still unaccounted for, a few more layers of the onion to be peeled off and more waves in the ocean to ride, but it has gotten easier, lighter, and more fun, with fewer and fewer attachments to outcomes. I notice whenever I happen to see a glimpse of myself in my rearview mirror that I have a perpetual smile. I also notice that I am very often blissful for absolutely no reason at all.

I feel so blessed to have had so many experiences that brought me closer and closer to who I am today. Looking back, I was a classic victim for the first half of my life and *very* gradually, after a gazillion mistakes, failures, and victories and never giving up, I miraculously awoke one day with a stronger sense of self-worth. Yes, I am that LSD lady in the flowing rainbow dress, but instead of descending the giant staircase, I'm now ascending: my higher self merged with my earthly self.

Nichiren Shoshu Buddhism (Soka Gakkai International) was my first adventure into spirituality. It taught me many things, one of which is being acutely aware of all the *miracles* that happen daily in my life with or without chanting. I notice that I've naturally come to expect miracles for almost everything every day. It taught me *compassion* for my members and *courage* to go outside my comfort zone and approach complete strangers in a personal and caring way. This has served me well as an Uber driver. My passengers sometimes read out loud the compliments other passengers have written about me on the app. One such quote gave me goosebumps: *"Yamini was the coolest and most badass Uber driver ever!"* I don't know who wrote this, but I have to say it made me feel like a millennial, not a senior citizen. Most all of my compliments are about my ability to connect in a meaningful and entertaining way. My navigation skills are not so good, perhaps because I talk *too* much, sometimes missing my turns. But no one has complained about that . . . yet.

Chanting two to three hours a day for thirteen years straight taught me *discipline* and *perseverance*. Discipline was in full bloom back then, but noticing my tendency toward procrastination these days, it could still use some tweaking. However, I can be proud of my perseverance through all the careers I've taken on. I seemed to have had no fear going up to movie stars at an event and asking to photograph them for my book *The Natural Goddess* or contacting well-known celebrities to speak at my Festival of Goddesses for free for three years. I believe this courage came from going out on the streets every night and inviting strangers to come to our Buddhist meetings.

One of my most important lessons was learning to *surrender* my ego and my many preconditioned opinions in order to trust and follow the guidance of a wiser, more experienced person than myself. I also learned the joy of *teamwork* in helping to create district meetings or huge theatrical events. During this time I put these lessons to good use, first as a social worker in LA and later as a wardrobe coordinator/designer, being an important part of many TV and movie production teams. It also served me later as a producer and creator of my own festivals.

But in spite of that, I still clung to my victimhood mentality in regard to relationships, which got amplified and then completely dismantled during my time with Osho.

Meditation practices through Osho brought me closer to my *divine authentic self*, which is pure bliss for no reason. With Bhagwan, I learned to be in the *here and now* (i.e., the *holy present*).

Some time ago, I visited a dear friend who was deeply depressed and suicidal and was put in a psyche ward to protect and prevent him from doing any harm to himself. While there, I read a passage to him from Osho's book *Ancient Music in the Pines*, which spoke of hope and hopelessness as living only in the future, not the present. Being a sannyasin himself, he listened attentively and understood.

"*So, you have lived with hope—now the hope has failed and you are living in hopelessness. Let the hopelessness also fail and drop hope and hopelessness together. Live here now! Living in hope is living in the future, which is really postponing life. It is not a way of living, but a way of suicide. There is no need to feel hopeless. Live here now! Life is tremendously blissful. It is showering here and you are looking somewhere else. It is just in front of your eyes, but your eyes have moved far away, they look at the horizon.*"

So Osho was there in that *here and now*, guiding my friend back to himself.

That book was pure magic. And so is this book. I thought I was nearly done writing when, shortly after my visit, I attended a party in celebration of my suicidal friend, who recovered completely. When he returned home, he and his wife gave a celebration party thanking all his friends for being there for him in his darkest hour. We all partook in our own transformation ceremony, releasing old wounds and habits and declaring our intentions going forward.

When I arrived at the house earlier, I saw someone running toward me with open arms, and dear God, it was VJ! We hugged and cried and said we loved each other, and I felt all the cells of my body wake up and align in jubilation to this unexpected reunion. She mentioned that because her daughter was being treated radically for breast cancer, she realized life was too short to carry any resentment and separate herself from her friends. Hallelujah! I had the very same thought months ago!

PING! Well, I'll be . . . a rider request came from someone named Lorelei in Pac Heights. Yes, it was the copper-haired beauty who transformed herself in the back seat of my car and then stepped blithely into a black hole on Broadway over a year ago. I hardly recognized her with her stylish hairdo cut an inch or two above her shoulders, parted on the side with a slant of hair falling over one eye. But she recognized me immediately and clapped her hands in glee. She informed me that what I told her the day of her audition was auspicious, because sure enough, she was challenged with the very things I warned her about. This made me so happy, and I asked her how her life had been since then. She thrust her left hand over the front seat and flashed a big diamond ring. This was not what I was expecting, but I saw the glow on her face and realized this meant everything to her. I congratulated her, and being mindful not to spoil the moment, I discreetly asked her about her singing career. Nodding her head with a resigned sigh, she related how she'd come to some harsh realizations about life in showbiz and decided that she wanted no part of it. Instead she landed a job in marketing and communications for one of San Francisco's famous art museums through some connections she'd made socially in San Francisco. This was where she'd met her fiancé. Softly she started singing a lullaby and patting her stomach, hoping to get my attention with a wistful smile. Catching her look through the rearview mirror, I thought, *Uh-huh . . . now that is excellent use of her talent!* I smiled back.

Recently I took a trip to Laguna and to my cousin Karla's wedding in Avalon, Catalina. Karla is in her sixties and has been single for the last thirty years after a failed marriage and two beautiful grown daughters. I've always thought of her as an earth angel with her long flowing blond hair and large doe-like eyes and mostly her very sweet demeanor. She found someone who recognized how special she is. This was a victory lap for her, and for me, a catalyst for another epiphany. I was witness to the purest and most profound expression of love between two people for a whole day and night. I felt saturated with their love.

However, the next morning I awoke with the inevitable "Why not me God?" So I prayed. I asked God to help me understand, to accept and to appreciate my station in life. What came up for me immediately, to my surprise, was my father. Unexpectedly, I saw a whole new rendition of my dad: the incorrigible egoist and womanizer suddenly had a big heart. I saw all the things he did to make me happy and to gain my love and respect. I saw that he knew I had lost respect for him after all the things I caught him doing with other women. He was besieged with a desperate need for my love and acceptance, especially when I entered my teens. This experience went beyond forgiveness as I realized there was nothing to forgive except my own entrenched and misguided beliefs. I cried tears of love for him as I let go of all those old worn-out stories that had kept me locked up in my own little prison.

Maybe more importantly, I have come to the understanding that being single is not the anathema it is made out to be in our culture. The accomplished single women who come to mind are Marianne Williamson, Oprah, Shirley MacLaine, Susan Sarandon, Diane Keaton, Katherine Hepburn, and Chelsea Handler who once said:

"It's not just O.K. to be single for both men and women — it's wonderful to be single, and society needs to embrace singlehood in all its splendiferous, solitary glory. Next time you see a single woman, instead of asking her where her boyfriend, husband or eunuch is, congratulate her on her accomplished sense of self and for reaching the solitary

mountaintop by herself without a ring on her finger weighing her down like a male paperweight. Without single women and their impressive sense of self, we'd be without Queen Elizabeth I, Susan B. Anthony, Florence Nightingale, Jane Austen, Harper Lee, Diane Keaton, Greta Garbo, Jane Goodall and me, myself and I. Being single is delightfully more than it's cracked up to be . . . if you can stand the horror of your own company, that is."

—Chelsea Handler featured in Vulture, 2013

Another leg of this trip took me to Temecula to visit my brother, a Trump follower, whom I hadn't seen for five years. I was mildly concerned and not quite sure what to expect. When I arrived, rather than the open-armed greeting that I had received many times in the past, he was noticeably wary. Our last political encounter was during the Obama administration, when he railed against him and spouted all kinds of conspiracy theories. I reacted as the passionate, progressive Obama lover I am and was shouted down. When I'm angry or confronted angrily, I lose my ability to argue coherently. So we had stayed away from each other except for sending cards and gifts at birthdays and Christmas. He never told me he voted for Trump, I just knew it, and it became obvious that trip. However, something in me was determined to heal this relationship and to gain his trust. The only way I felt I could do that was to not judge him but to just love and appreciate him and avoid any political discussion. It worked. He did try a couple of times, and I would either just smile and nod or change the subject to a more personal one that he could respond to positively. He once mentioned something about "fake news" from the *New York Times* and so on, and I just opined that all journalists are human and tend to be slanted one way or another. Fox News and Trump were never mentioned.

And then I took a trip to Tacoma, Washington, to attend another wedding: my godson's. There, miles away from home, a very strange thing happened. With 150 of their young friends dressed in Roaring Twenties costumes (me and his mom included), as per the couple's request, we took part in the celebration. The wedding was lively and joyous, and my little godson was now a grown man, and a husband to boot. At the reception, his bride decided to throw her bouquet. I saw about twenty of her girlfriends rush to the front of the room as I sat there, sipping Champaign bemusedly, when suddenly, several of the girls turned to face me and pointed a finger, signaling me to join them. I shook my head and made a big X with my fingers, but they wouldn't stop. I didn't want to make a big deal of it, so I surrendered and was sauntering up there when someone grabbed my arm and pulled me to the front and center of the lineup. And then it happened: the bouquet was lobbed, falling in slow motion from a high arch, and landed squarely and uncontestably in my hands, which were waist level, not over my head in the usual anticipatory stance. Whaaaa?! This had *never* happened. Why now?

Getting back to my time with Bhagwan and the many insights he thrust into my consciousness: I learned how to tap into my *authentic* self through heart connections, creativity, and meditation. I think I was able to demonstrate "lesson learned" with my brother. Another lesson Bhagwan pounded into our heads was letting go of *attachment* to anything and everything (especially to him). With my brother, I was able to let go of my need to be right and my attachment to my political beliefs. The payoff is love and connection. The payoff to being right is the illusion of superiority and ultimately separation and regret. I feel the trust I was able to engender between us has laid the groundwork for future conversations. Perhaps we will be able to argue for our POV with each other in a respectful, harmonious, and loving way, no matter what the topic.

However, I'm not sure what this bouquet thing is all about. Is it attachment to a myth or belief perpetrated by a centuries-old tradition? Is there any merit to this, or should I take it with a grain of salt?

Actually, it reminds me of the time I found a beautiful orchid lei in the back of my truck, and I imagined it was a gift from Bhagwan. There was no other reason for a tropical lei to be anywhere near the ranch in Central Oregon, much less in my truck. I felt it was a sign of acknowledgment and love.

Osho demonstrated the absurdity of attachment on a very visceral level by flaunting his ninety-three Rolls-Royces, which were given to him by his wealthiest sannyasins, who adored him and wanted to give him the best. And what better way to reach people than through the media, which went bananas over the news about his ridiculous number of Rolls-Royces in this age of rampant consumerism? It is more than likely that he was conspiring to transcend his silence and isolation in Central Oregon by doing something so outrageous that people's curiosity would lead them to his teachings. I don't think it's an accident that thirty-six years later, a documentary on Osho and his followers in Oregon was shown at the Sundance Film Festival and became a popular Netflix series on TV called *Wild Wild Country*.

I also learned that my *body* is a *temple* to be nurtured with organic healthy food, rest, exercise, and an implicit understanding of its *sexual function* in *relationships*. Tantric sex takes it to another level of deep resonance with myself and with my partner (whoever it is at the time). With it, I became *unashamed* of my body. It is a gift, after all, and I must honor it as such. In addition to that, I acquired the ability to treat everything as a *meditation* (e.g., driving, cooking, washing dishes, sweeping floors, making my bed, or dancing). It's all done with mindfulness, as if painting a masterpiece

And finally, I learned that *I am the master* of my life and the final authority. With Bhagwan's guidance I have become a *light unto myself*!

And then there's people like Katherine Woodward Thomas, Marianne Williamson, Deepak Chopra, Michael Bernard Beckwith, Ram Dass, Neale Donald Walsch, Eckart Tolle, Matt Kahn, Paul Selig, Brene Brown, and a plethora of other spiritual leaders who have shaped my beliefs and guided my journey into and through the unknown.

Throughout my spiritual journey, I was able to step outside my comfort zone and explore exciting new worlds and innately feel that I belonged there. The road was never in a straight line. There were dips and curves and roundabouts that looped me back to the land of victimhood from time to time until I had wiped all the capital letters of VICTIMHOOD off the screen, leaving only a faint reminder of it in lower-case size-8 font.

I now seem to have a certain resiliency and acceptance of *what is*, no matter how dire or strange the circumstances appear to be. It stems from a deep connection I feel to everyone and everything. I even began talking gently to my hair yesterday, encouraging it to stay in place, as if it were a little being that needed coddling. I talk to all my potted plants every day, certain that they know and appreciate everything I say to them. I'm sure that's why they are so healthy.

I'm also noticing how *everything* in my life *flows*, particularly when I am aligned with my higher self by thought or by declaration. Occasionally, there's a blip on my screen, but enough money is always in my bank account, and time seems to be on my side no matter how late I think I'm going to be. I either arrive on time *or* everyone else is late *or* it doesn't matter. Also, while Uber driving in heavy, frenetic traffic in San Francisco, I'm not the least affected by it. I just move at an even pace and always arrive safely and on time for my passengers. Also, when I least expect it, someone comes into my life who becomes a catalyst, either for an endearing friendship, a promising future, or for further illumination. There is no one in my life now who is dissonant to my well-being, including myself. In fact, I see love coming at me from all sides, like many brothers and sisters with open arms. "I see with the *eyes* of *Christ*," so what or who could possibly be bad or wrong or ugly?

Yes, it was a wild ride that has landed in a field of clover. Imagine, if you can, a seventy-nine-year-old woman rolling around unashamedly, whooping and hollering in the clover. Keep that image in your mind as you read on:

PING! I was ready to go home when this request came in before I had a chance to turn the Uber app off. I was summoned to the corner of Harbor and Bridgeway in Sausalito, where someone stood whom I recognized from my Sunday Sweat Your Prayers dance. When I approached more closely, he showed surprise that I was his Uber driver and started to open the door to the back but then decided to sit up front with me. He was a good-looking older guy, tall and slim with straight blond-white hair and soulful brown eyes, which he fixed on mine for what seemed like an eternity.

Feeling somewhat shaken, I told myself that this was a common greeting in our community, and I really shouldn't think anything of it except that it's a soulful acknowledgment between friends. We had never spoken before at the Sunday dance (talking on the dance floor is prohibited, as this is a form of meditation), but we did have a sweet connection while dancing, which I remembered quite vividly. So we introduced ourselves, and something about him made me laugh and say the silliest things. I liked who I was being with him, and I felt like I had known him a long time. We laughed about nothing in particular all the way to his house. And yes, that sapphire-blue Tesla did cross my mind, not to mention the wedding bouquet I unexpectedly caught two months prior.

When he let himself out, he came around to my side and motioned for me to open the door and get out. Following his lead, I stepped out and somehow landed in his arms in a warm, lingering hug. I thought, *Mmmmmm, how nice it would be to meet again at Sweat Your Prayers.*

And so we did.

ACKNOWLEDGMENTS

First and foremost, I want to acknowledge all the Bay Area Uber riders who have inspired and supported me on my journey. Our brief but powerful encounters mean more to me than you will ever know.

Of course I am so thankful to all those talented and loving souls who supported the writing and production of this book, including Brooke Warner and Cait Levin of She Writes Press. Brooke goes above and beyond as a publisher, supporting her authors in a profound and proactive way.

Special thanks to Jill Lublin, Michel Joy DelRe, and Geoff Affleck for their expert consulting and publicity training. Thanks to Gail Watson and Laura Rubenstien from Women's Speaker Association for their expert video speech training. Kudos to Randy Peyser and Anila Manning for all their hard work editing and proofreading my book. Thanks to Susan Tracy from PR Leads and Jane Richey, my talented portrait photographer. And thanks to Kay Leroy from Book Passage in Marin for believing in my book enough to host my launch at the store in the Ferry Building in San Francisco.

I so appreciate the support given me by Kelly Sullivan Walden all these years for both my books and to Katherine Woodward Thomas,

Marci Shimoff, Agapi Stassinopoulos, Judee Morton Fraser, and others already mentioned for their endorsements. Thanks also to Avinasho and Dhanyam from Osho Viha. I must also mention the loving support from many dear friends: Nicola Amadora, Rama Gifford, Christy Michaels, Angel B. Nei, Dawn Jackson, Lori and Rollie Bennett, Rajyo and Vinit Allen, David and Andrea Lieberstein, Quana Ryals and Doug Waagen, and my daughter, Molly.

Finally, deep appreciation for the wisdom and loving support of my Ascended Masters book club and for the wisdom from my longtime Spiritual Master, Osho.

ABOUT THE AUTHOR

Born Frances Hamilton Redewill in 1939 in Oakland, CA, Yamini Redewill was given the name Ma Veet Yamini, meaning "going beyond the night," by Bhagwan Shree Rashneesh in India in 1981. Redewill attended UC Berkeley and graduated with a BA in Fine Arts from UCLA in 1964. After first pursuing a career in acting and singing, she later rose to prominence as the head of wardrobe at CBS-TV and later as a freelance costumer and designer at various Hollywood studios. She later became a photographer and women's empowerment advocate who created a new niche in photography with her Natural Goddess portraits of women over forty in nature. In 2014, Redewill compiled her best goddess portraits into a self-published book called *The Natural Goddess: Portraits of True Beauty in Women Over 40*, which included portraits of Diane Ladd, Connie Stevens, Marla Maples, and Stephanie Powers, along with such notable authors as Barbara Marx Hubbard, Ariel Ford, Lynn Andrews and others.

SELECTED TITLES FROM SHE WRITES PRESS

She Writes Press is an independent publishing company founded to serve women writers everywhere. Visit us at www.shewritespress.com.

Operatic Divas and Naked Irishmen: An Innkeeper's Tale by Nancy R. Hinchliff. $16.95, 978-1-63152-194-2

At sixty four, divorced, retired, and with no prior business experience and little start-up money, Nancy Hinchliff impulsively moves to a new city where she knows only one person, buys a 125-year-old historic mansion, and turns it into a bed and breakfast.

Daring to Date Again: A Memoir by Ann Anderson Evans. $16.95, 978-1-63152-909-2

A hilarious, no-holds-barred memoir about a legal secretary turned professor who dives back into the dating pool headfirst after twelve years of celibacy.

Not a Perfect Fit: Stories from Jane's World by Jane A. Schmidt. $16.95, 978-1631522062

Jane Schmidt documents her challenges living off grid, moving from the city to the country, living with a variety of animals as her only companions, dating, family trips, outdoor adventures, and midlife in essays full of honesty and humor.

Gap Year Girl by Marianne Bohr. $16.95, 978-1-63152-820-0

Thirty-plus years after first backpacking through Europe, Marianne Bohr and her husband leave their lives behind and take off on a yearlong quest for adventure.

Naked Mountain: A Memoir by Marcia Mabee. $16.95, 978-1-63152-097-6

A compelling memoir of one woman's journey of natural world discovery, tragedy, and the enduring bonds of marriage, set against the backdrop of a stunning mountaintop in rural Virginia.

Postcards from the Sky: Adventures of an Aviatrix by Erin Seidemann. $16.95, 978-1-63152-826-2

Erin Seidemann's tales of her her struggles, adventures, and relationships as a woman making her way in a world very much dominated by men: aviation.